# Classic
# Rock Climbs <sup>No. 28</sup>

# Red Rocks
## Nevada

Todd Swain

CHOCKSTONE®

FALCON®

# A FALCON GUIDE®

Falcon® Publishing is continually expanding its list of recreation guidebooks. All books include detailed descriptions, accurate maps, and all the information necessary for enjoyable trips. You can order extra copies of this book and get information and prices for other Falcon® guidebooks by writing The Globe Pequot Press, P.O. Box 480, Guilford, Connecticut 06437 or calling toll free 1-800-582-2665. Also, please ask for a free copy of our current catalog. Visit our website at www.Falcon.com or contact us by e-mail at falcon@falcon.com.

Printed in the United States of America

1 2 3 4 5 6 7 8 9 0 MG 06 05 04 03 02 01

Cover photo of climber leading on *Fear and Loathing* by Alan Kearney/The Viesti Collection.

Cataloging-in-Publication Data is on file at the Library of Congress.

**CAUTION**

Outdoor recreational activities are by their very nature potentially hazardous. All participants in such activities must assume the responsibility for their own actions and safety. The information contained in this guidebook cannot replace sound judgment and good decision-making skills, which help reduce risk exposure, nor does the scope of this book allow for disclosure of all the potential hazards and risks involved in such activities.

Learn as much as possible about the outdoor recreational activities in which you participate, prepare for the unexpected, and be cautious. The reward will be a safer and more enjoyable experience.

 Text pages printed on recycled paper.

# WARNING:
## CLIMBING IS A SPORT WHERE YOU MAY BE SERIOUSLY INJURED OR DIE. READ THIS BEFORE YOU USE THIS BOOK.

This guidebook is a compilation of unverified information gathered from many different climbers. The author cannot assure the accuracy of any of the information in this book, including the topos and route descriptions, the difficulty ratings, and the protection ratings. These may be incorrect or misleading and it is impossible for any one author to climb all the routes to confirm the information about each route. Also, ratings of climbing difficulty and danger are always subjective and depend on the physical characteristics (for example, height), experience, technical ability, confidence and physical fitness of the climber who supplied the rating. Additionally, climbers who achieve first ascents sometimes underrate the difficulty or danger of the climbing route out of fear of being ridiculed if a climb is later down-rated by subsequent ascents. Therefore, be warned that you must exercise your own judgment on where a climbing route goes, its difficulty and your ability to safely protect yourself from the risks of rock climbing. Examples of some of these risks are: falling due to technical difficulty or due to natural hazards such as holds breaking, falling rock, climbing equipment dropped by other climbers, hazards of weather and lightning, your own equipment failure, and failure or absence of fixed protection.

**You should not depend on any information gleaned from this book for your personal safety; your safety depends on your own good judgment, based on experience and a realistic assessment of your climbing ability. If you have any doubt as to your ability to safely climb a route described in this book, do not attempt it.**

The following are some ways to make your use of this book safer:

**1. Consultation:** You should consult with other climbers about the difficulty and danger of a particular climb prior to attempting it. Most local climbers are glad to give advice on routes in their area and we suggest that you contact locals to confirm ratings and safety of particular routes and to obtain first-hand information about a route chosen from this book.

**2. Instruction:** Most climbing areas have local climbing instructors and guides available. We recommend that you engage an instructor or guide to learn safety techniques and to become familiar with the routes and hazards of the areas described in this book. Even after you are proficient in climbing safely, occasional use of a guide is a safe way to raise your climbing standard and learn advanced techniques.

**3. Fixed Protection:** Many of the routes in this book use bolts and pitons which are permanently placed in the rock. Because of variances in the manner of placement, weathering, metal fatigue, the quality of the metal used, and many other factors, these fixed protection pieces should always be considered suspect and should always be backed up by equipment that you place yourself. Never depend for your safety on a single piece of fixed protection because you never can tell whether it will hold weight, and in some cases, fixed protection may have been removed or is now absent.

Be aware of the following specific potential hazards which could arise in using this book:

**1. Misdescriptions of Routes:** If you climb a route and you have a doubt as to where the route may go, you should not go on unless you are sure that you can go that way safely. Route descriptions and topos in this book may be inaccurate or misleading.

**2. Incorrect Difficulty Rating:** A route may, in fact, be more difficult than the rating indicates. Do not be lulled into a false sense of security by the difficulty rating.

**3. Incorrect Protection Rating:** If you climb a route and you are unable to arrange adequate protection from the risk of falling through the use of fixed pitons or bolts and by placing your own protection devices, do not assume that there is adequate protection available higher just because the route protection rating indicates the route is not an "X" or an "R" rating. Every route is potentially an "X" (a fall may be deadly), due to the inherent hazards of climbing – including, for example, failure or absence of fixed protection, your own equipment's failure, or improper use of climbing equipment.

THERE ARE NO WARRANTIES, WHETHER EXPRESS OR IMPLIED, THAT THIS GUIDEBOOK IS ACCURATE OR THAT THE INFORMATION CONTAINED IN IT IS RELIABLE. THERE ARE NO WARRANTIES OF FITNESS FOR A PARTICULAR PURPOSE OR THAT THIS GUIDE IS MERCHANTABLE. YOUR USE OF THIS BOOK INDICATES YOUR ASSUMPTION OF THE RISK THAT IT MAY CONTAIN ERRORS AND IS AN ACKNOWLEDGMENT OF YOUR OWN SOLE RESPONSIBILITY FOR YOUR CLIMBING SAFETY.

# CONTENTS

## GREATER LAS VEGAS
## (MAP NOT TO SCALE)

# RED ROCKS
## (MAP NOT TO SCALE)

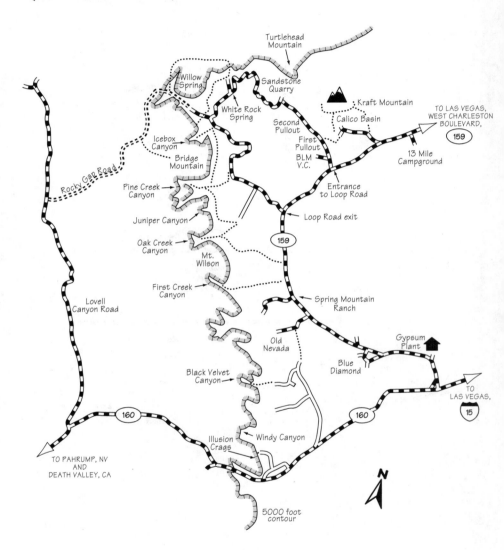

Turtlehead Mountain

Willow Spring

Sandstone Quarry

White Rock Spring

Kraft Mountain

TO LAS VEGAS, WEST CHARLESTON BOULEVARD, 159

Calico Basin

Second Pullout

First Pullout BLM V.C.

13 Mile Campground

Icebox Canyon

Bridge Mountain

Rocky Gap Road

Pine Creek Canyon

Entrance to Loop Road

Loop Road exit

Juniper Canyon

159

Oak Creek Canyon

Mt. Wilson

First Creek Canyon

Spring Mountain Ranch

Lovell Canyon Road

Old Nevada

Gypsum Plant

Black Velvet Canyon

Blue Diamond

160

TO LAS VEGAS, 15

TO PAHRUMP, NV AND DEATH VALLEY, CA

Illusion Crags

Windy Canyon

160

5000 foot contour

N

## MAP LEGEND

Trail

Interstate

Paved Road

Gravel Road

Unimproved Road

State Line, Forest, Park, or Wilderness Boundary

Waterway

Intermittent Waterway

Lake/Reservoir

Building

Camping

Gate

Town

City

Climbing Area

Crag/Boulder

Cliff Edge

Mountain Peak

Trailhead

Parking

Interstate

U.S. Highway

State Highway

County Road

Forest Road

Mile Marker

**KEY TO TOPO DRAWINGS**

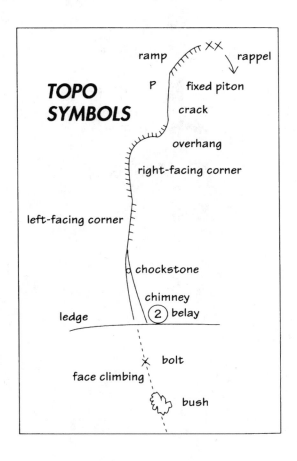

INTRODUCTION

# Red Rocks

Most climbers have now at least heard of Red Rocks and know that it lies just outside of Las Vegas, Nevada.

The area hosts numerous climbs of world-class stature. The area is officially named Red Rock Canyon National Conservation Area and is administered by the Bureau of Land Management (BLM), a federal agency within the United States Department of the Interior.

**GETTING THERE**   Once you arrive in Las Vegas, you'll find that it's pretty simple to get around. McCarran Airport is right off the Strip, while Interstate 15 and U.S. Highway 93/95 divide the city roughly into quarters. The Red Rock escarpment is located about 15 miles west of Las Vegas and is typically approached from West Charleston Boulevard (Nevada 159).

With the exception of Black Velvet Canyon, all of the climbing at Red Rocks included in this book is accessed by NV 159 and a one-way scenic loop road. This loop road, within the National Conservation Area (NCA), is gated and closed at night. Typically, the road is open from early morning until just after dark. An entrance fee is required to use the loop road and Red Spring Area of the NCA. Check with the NCA Visitor Center or local climbing shops for current opening and closing times. Black Velvet Canyon is accessed via NV 160.

The introduction to each chapter of this guide describes how to get to the trailhead for that certain area. The individual route descriptions tell you how to get from your car to the base of the climb. Hiking approach times at Red Rocks range from a few minutes to four hours and are also mentioned in the chapter and route introductions.

**THE LAND**   Like all climbing areas, Red Rock Canyon National Conservation Area should be treated with the utmost respect. The area was first designated as Red Rock Canyon Recreation Lands in 1967, and the scenic loop road was completed in 1978.

The current designation as a National Conservation Area came in 1990. It is defined as "An area of the public lands managed by the Bureau of Land Management which has been established by Congress for the purpose of protecting and conserving identified resource values of national interest. A Conservation Area is managed for multiple use and sustained yield in conformance with the Resource Management Plan and in accordance with a General Management Plan which reflects the dominant and compatible uses for specific tracts."

Red Rock Canyon NCA currently encompasses 196,000 acres and hosts nearly one million visitors each year. A very nice visitor center located just off the scenic loop road has interpretive displays, books, postcards, and a helpful staff. The visitor center is typically open from 8:30 a.m. to 4:30 p.m. For more information, call 702-363-1921.

The BLM has a number of useful handouts for planning your visit to Red Rocks. These include a park brochure and the following titles: *Climbing and Camping, Hiking, Mammals, Birds, Geology, Plants,* and *Archeology of Southern Nevada.* For more information, brochures, or a list of other publications available, contact the BLM at Las Vegas District Office, 4765 West Vegas Drive, Las Vegas, NV 89108; 702-647-5000.

**REGULATIONS** As climber visitation increases, land managers at Red Rocks and other desert parks are becoming more concerned about a number of climbing impacts. Please abide by posted regulations and closure times, and be courteous to other user groups. The following climbing-related regulations are currently in effect at Red Rock Canyon National Conservation Area. (Note: The first three regulations are extremely important. Violations will most likely lead to the closure of climbing areas.)

- It is prohibited to chip, chisel, glue, or scar the rock.
- Climbing is not allowed within 50 feet of any Native American rock art site (petroglyphs and/or pictographs).
- Digging or in any way disturbing archaeological sites is prohibited.
- Camping is allowed only in designated camping areas, or, when backpacking, above 5,000 feet elevation (accessed only off the Red Rock Summit Road/ Rocky Gap Road or Lovell Canyon Road). When backpacking, you must camp more than 200 feet from archaeological sites and water sources. **Note:** As of press time, roadside camping was only allowed at 13 Mile Campground.
- Vehicles must be outside the gated sections of the loop road before closing time. (If there's one thing that annoys the rangers at Red Rocks, it's waiting for tardy visitors to get back to their cars and exit the loop road.)
- Permits are required for backpacking, bivouacs, and early or late access to the loop road. Contact the NCA Visitor Center for more details.
- Fires are allowed only within furnished fire grates.
- Gathering of native vegetation is prohibited. Bring your own firewood.

**LOW IMPACT**  In addition, a number of very important low impact policies should be followed.

- Do not climb on wet sandstone! The rock becomes very brittle and typically needs at least 24 hours to dry.
- Pack out all trash, whether it's yours or not.
- Pack out all toilet paper and human waste using a Ziploc-type bag. At the least, bury waste 6 inches deep and always carry out toilet paper.
- Stay on maintained trails as much as possible and try to minimize impacts to plants and soil through erosion and trampling.
- New routes should be established away from the view of the general public. At Sandstone Quarry no new fixed anchors are allowed within 0.25 mile of the parking area.
- All bolts and anchors should be painted to match the color of the rock. If webbing is used, it should also match the color of the rock.
- To help keep the visual impacts of climbing to a minimum, remove all retreat (or bail) slings you encounter.
- Do not use chalk on areas visible to the general public. This definitely applies to the boulders at Willow Spring Picnic Area and Sandstone Quarry.

**THE RULES OF THE GAME**  How a route is established (whether from the ground up or on rappel) will never be as important as having the opportunity to climb. Do your part to minimize all impacts associated with climbing (noise, visuals, social trails, human waste, disturbing wildlife, etc.). Climb to have fun, not to aggravate others or upset land managers.

**RATINGS**  The Yosemite Decimal System (YDS) is used throughout this book to rate climbs. Currently, technical rock climbs at Red Rocks range from 5.0 to 5.13. The higher the number, the more difficult the climb. Aid ratings go from A0 (tension or grabbing a sling) to A5 (long stretches of body-weight-only placements). To differentiate between true sport climbs (quickdraws only) and routes where gear is needed, I have used two different types of subgrading methods.

True sport climbs have ratings subdivided by letter grades (a–d), as was introduced by Jim Bridwell of Yosemite fame. Routes that require some amount of traditional gear have the subdivisions of minus and plus. These "gear subdivisions" are used on climbs 5.10 or harder, with a rating of 5.10- being equal in difficulty to 5.10a.

As with any rating system, the ratings are not meant to be definitive but are intended to give you a rough idea of the difficulty that may be encountered. Height, reach, finger size, and flexibility vary for each climber, thus making the rating system somewhat inaccurate. Just because a route is rated 5.9 doesn't mean it's really 5.9. Remember, I haven't done all of the routes in this guide; therefore, the information should be considered suspect.

I also have used the protection rating system first introduced by Jim Erickson in his climbing guide to Boulder, Colorado. This system is based on the movie rating system (G, PG, PG13, R, and X), with X-rated routes being very dangerous. There may be very dangerous climbs listed in this book that don't have an R or X rating. Use caution and good judgment when leading!

I have dropped the G ("safe") rating and use only the other four grades. These ratings assume the leader is competent at the grade, has the proper equipment for the route, and has an attentive belayer. Roughly, the ratings mean:

**PG**      Protection is usually considered adequate, although the leader may fall up to 15 feet. The leader will probably not get injured in the fall. These routes might seem a little bit sporty.

**PG13**   This is somewhere between PG and R (as you might have guessed).

**R**       Protection is usually considered inadequate and the leader will probably get injured if he/she falls. These routes are potentially dangerous and runout.

**X**       Protection is nonexistent. A falling leader will probably suffer severe injuries and/or death. These are death routes or solos.

**GEAR**   The joy of sport climbing is that you need only a rope, quickdraws, and strong fingers. For the traditional routes, you'll want a good selection of wires, TCUs, Friends, and slings. "Specialty" gear is noted in the description of the climb. For the longer canyon routes, you'll usually need two ropes to descend. Again, this is noted in the description.

**WEATHER**   Climbing is possible at Red Rocks all year, but most people visit the area in the spring and fall. Red Rocks is generally cooler and wetter than Joshua Tree. For the latest forecast, check out the numerous weather sites on the Internet. The preferred weather telephone number is 702-736-3854. You can also call 702-734-2010. "Typical" weather for each season is detailed below.

**Spring:** While the weather can be good, it's likely that there will be windy and wet conditions in March. Shade combined with down-canyon winds can make places like Black Velvet seem much colder than the sunny cliffs of the Calico Hills. By May, the temperatures could reach 100 degrees Fahrenheit (F).

**Summer:** It is common for temperatures to reach 106 degrees F or higher. Thunderstorms are the norm for late July and all of August, and these rains frequently cause flash floods. Climb in the early morning and evening hours, and avoid the sun. Drink lots of water!

**Fall:** Although the days are getting shorter, it is probably the best time to visit the area. As November rolls around, expect it to get cold in the shady canyons. Places like The Gallery are warm enough for climbing in shorts and T-shirts.

**Winter:** Sunny cliffs, such as The Gallery and Trophy, are extremely popular. Snow is common at the higher elevations and forces the closure of the loop road on occasion. Shady canyon climbs are usually out of the question. Shaded descents (such as on *Solar Slab*) may remain icy for some time.

## Emergencies

The BLM and Las Vegas Metropolitan Police Department (Metro) provide emergency services at Red Rocks. Emergency telephones are located on the scenic loop road at Sandstone Quarry, White Rock Spring, and Icebox Canyon. Between 8 a.m. and 5 p.m., report the accident to the NCA Visitor Center if possible. After hours, call from pay phones at the entrance to the loop road, outside the NCA Visitor Center, or in the towns of Blue Diamond, Old Nevada (Bonnie Springs Ranch), and Las Vegas.

Emergency Telephone Numbers:

- BLM Emergency Dispatch: 702-293-8932
- Las Vegas Metropolitan Police: 911
- BLM Non-Emergency Dispatch: 702-293-8998
- NCA Visitor Center: 702-363-1921

**Area Medical Facilities:** The nearest hospital to the crags is Summerlin Medical Center (655 Town Center Drive; 702-233-7000). Head into town on West Charleston and turn left (north) on Hualapai Way. The hospital is about 1 mile north on Hualapai Way and is visible from West Charleston. It is a multistoried tan building on the northeast side of a traffic circle. Other local hospitals include University Medical Center (1800 West Charleston; 702-383-2000) and Valley Hospital Medical Center (620 Shadow Lane; 702-388-4000). Valley Hospital has Flight for Life capabilities.

## Where to Stay

Las Vegas has over 120,000 rooms available for its 32 million annual visitors. These rooms range from astonishingly cheap to astronomically expensive. Many of the huge casinos on The Strip offer great deals and are only minutes away from the crags. As a general rule, room prices are quite a bit higher on weekends and in the summer. At least one hotel offers discounts to climbers. Check with the climbing shops or local Internet sites for details.

For those who want to camp, the choices are very limited. As of September 2000, 13 Mile Campground was the only convenient place to legally camp. This BLM campground is located on West Charleston (Nevada 159), roughly 1 mile east (toward town) from Calico Basin Road. The campground currently has individual sites that cost $10 per night (limited to two vehicles), walk-in sites ($5 per night), and group sites ($25 a night). Long-range plans include as many as 10 group sites with several of these sites able to accommodate up to 50 people. The campground has drinking water and restrooms. Check with the BLM or local climbing shops for the latest information. There are also commercial campgrounds in Las Vegas, some of which will provide showers to those staying elsewhere.

## Supplies and Other Important Information

Along West Charleston (Nevada 159), you find grocery, drug, and department stores, as well as numerous restaurants. Blue Diamond has a small convenience store with limited items. Water is available at the NCA Visitor Center and at various places in town.

Numerous movie theaters can be found in the local area. The Red Rock Cinema is about 1 mile east of Rainbow at 5201 West Charleston (702-870-1423). The Torrey Pines Theater at 6344 West Sahara (the intersection of Torrey Pines) offers cheaper, second-run movies (702-876-4334). There is a public library at 6301 West Charleston, just west of Jones. There is also a small branch library in Blue Diamond.

Showers are available at some commercial campgrounds, climbing gyms, and fitness centers. Check with the local climbing shops for the latest information. Do not use the NCA Visitor Center bathrooms for bathing.

## Las Vegas

If you haven't been to Vegas yet, you're missing out! Before your trip, rent the following films at your local video store to get a feel for the area: *Bugsy* starring Warren Beatty, *Viva Las Vegas* starring Elvis, and *Honeymoon in Vegas* starring Nicholas Cage. Here's a list of my favorite things to show first-time visitors to Las Vegas.

**Bellagio:** The owners of this hotel intended it to be the most elegant in the world. If you can afford it, see the Cirque du Soleil show ($100/person), which features some amazing stuff. Several local climbers work as riggers on the show. Check out the free water fountain show in front of the casino as well.

**Caesar's Palace:** One of the more opulent casinos, you'll find a higher-class clientele here than at Circus, Circus. Take in a movie at the large-screen

Omnimax Theater and don't miss The Forum, an amazing shopping area featuring talking statues and a "sky" that changes.

**Coca Cola World:** Across from New York, New York and next to the MGM Grand is a relatively interesting complex featuring an indoor climbing wall (expensive), Coca Cola World, and M&M World (not worth it). Downstairs are more video games than you have ever seen before!

**Circus, Circus:** A bit tacky, but the original casino designed to suck in the whole family. Check out the free circus acts (running from about noon to midnight), the midway, and "The World's Largest Buffet." Grand Slam Canyon is attached to the rear of the casino and features an indoor roller coaster and other stuff.

**Excalibur:** The biggest (and gaudiest) hotel in the world when it was built. It sports a medieval motif and was built by Circus, Circus. For those with money ($25), the dinner theater features jousting and other knightly derring-do.

**"Glitter Gulch":** This is the downtown part of Vegas. The buildings generally aren't as tall as those on the Strip, but their closeness makes the neon that much more impressive.

**Las Vegas Hilton:** The *Star Trek* show is expensive, but a must for sci-fi fans.

**Luxor:** It's shaped like a pyramid and has an Egyptian theme. Sooner or later, I think someone will attempt to BASE jump the interior. Check out just the first Episode and the buffet.

**The Mirage:** There are a bunch of free things to experience here. Don't miss the exploding volcano in front of the casino. It erupts on a regular basis all evening. Inside, you find rare white tigers (usually sleeping), a tropical jungle, and a huge tropical aquarium (behind the check-in desk).

**MGM Grand:** This huge, green casino/outdoor amusement park is across the street from New York, New York. It has all sorts of shows and rides to while away those long winter nights but is barely worth the entrance fee.

**New York, New York:** An interesting and realistic exterior and interior (once you see them, you know what I mean). The roller coaster is worth the money.

**Treasure Island:** Don't miss the free pirate battle in front of the casino (run multiple times each evening if it isn't windy).

## Local Climbing Shops

Desert Rock Sports
8201 West Charleston Boulevard
Las Vegas, NV 89117
702-254-1143
www.desertrocksports.com

Great Basin Outdoors
2925 North Green Valley Parkway
Henderson, NV 89014
702-454-4997

## Local Authorized Guide Services

Jackson Hole Mountain Guides
P.O. Box 80875
Las Vegas, NV 89180
702-223-2176

Sky's The Limit
HCR 33 Box 1
Calico Basin, NV 89124-9209
702-363-4533
www.skysthelimit.com

Contact the BLM for other authorized guide services.

## Guidebooks

*Rock Climbing Red Rocks;* Falcon, spring 2000.
Contains more than 1,100 routes.

*Classic Rock Climbs No. 28: Red Rocks;* Falcon, spring 2001.
Contains 226 selected routes.

*The Red Rocks of Southern Nevada;* American Alpine, reprinted 1999.
Contains 220 traditional routes from the 1970s and '80s.

CHAPTER ONE

# Calico Basin

The Calico Basin is a portion of the conservation area that has many private residences. In the past few years, climbers have not been particularly sensitive to these residents, despite warnings in previous editions of this guidebook. Consequently, parking and access have become an issue. Please keep a very low profile and park only in authorized areas!

## Red Spring Area/Calico Basin South

The climbs in this chapter are in the area around Red Spring Picnic Area along the western side of the basin. This is a good area to visit if you don't want to drive the entire scenic loop road. To reach the picnic area, turn off West Charleston (Nevada 159) onto Calico Basin Road and follow it for 1.2 miles to a T-intersection. Turn left into the Red Spring Picnic Area and park.

### *Moderate Mecca*

This newly developed area has become quite popular due to the short approach and warmth. Park at the back (southern end) of the parking lot inside the Red Spring Picnic Area. Walk south up the obvious old road to the top of a dirt ridge (100 yards). Follow the road downhill into a valley for 20 yards, then angle right (west) onto a ledge that runs along the cliff (it'll seem like you're going to end up on top of the cliff). Routes are described from east (toward Las Vegas) to west as you encounter them. If you walk up the bottom of the valley, you'll eventually arrive at the First Pullout.

The following routes begin on the ledge system described in the approach to the area.

**1    Stew on This (5.10 PG)** Rope up about 250' from the right (east) edge of the formation at an arête on the main ledge system. Mantle past a low overhang (bolt) to a stance below a steep varnished wall (#2–2.5 cam placement). Climb the varnished face past a bolt to easier climbing on light-colored rock. There is an anchor on the arête above.

**2    Is It Soup Yet? (5.10 PG)** Start 10' left of the last route on the west side of the arête. Pull past a low ceiling (bolt) then up a steep, shallow dihedral to a

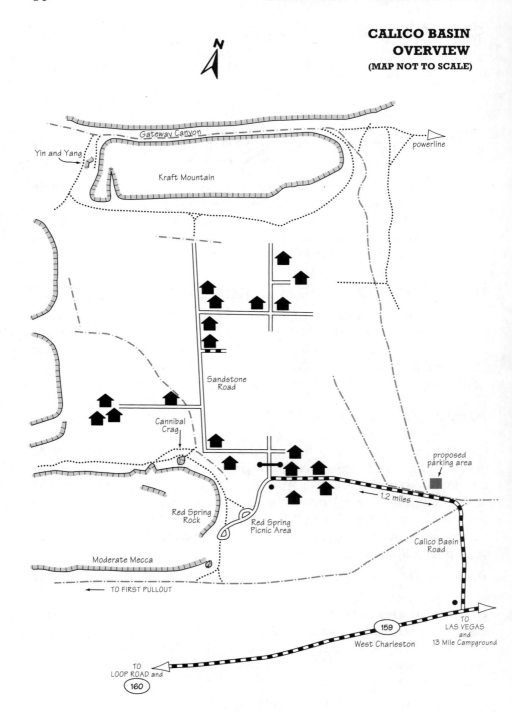

N

Gateway Canyon

powerline

Yin and Yang

Kraft Mountain

Sandstone
Road

Cannibal
Crag

proposed
parking area

1.2 miles

Red Spring
Rock

Red Spring
Picnic Area

Calico Basin
Road

Moderate Mecca

← TO FIRST PULLOUT

159

West Charleston

TO
LAS VEGAS
and
13 Mile Campground

TO
LOOP ROAD and
160

ledge. Continue up the short face to an anchor on the arête. Bring wires, TCUs, and small cams to protect the route.

**3    Chicken Soup for the Soul (5.10- TR)** Begin 10' left of the last route and just right of a large, left-facing corner. Climb the steep face past a shallow left-facing corner and huecos to the top. Medium cams and long slings needed for the anchor.

**4    Chicken Gumbo for Your Dumbo (5.6)** A good little route. Same start as the last route at a varnished, left-facing corner that is just right of the main corner. Climb the small, varnished corner to the top. Bring gear to a #3.5 Friend. Walk off right. (No topo.)

**5    Soupy Sales (5.6+)** Harder than it looks. Climb the obvious crack/left-facing corner (5' left of the last route) to the summit. (No topo.)

**6    From Soup to Nuts (5.7)** Ascend the crack 5' left of the last route. The crux is at the bottom. Bring gear to a #4 cam, including a #2.5 and #3 Friend for the anchor. Walk off right (east). (No topo.)

**7    The Singing Love Pen (5.9)** Rope up 30' left of the last route at the left side of a black face. The route starts at a right-facing corner and follows a crack through a bulge. Finish up a lower-angle crack to a right-facing corner. Bring equipment up to a #3.5 Friend. (No topo.)

**8    Valentine's Day (5.8+)** You'll love this one. Rope up 20' left of *The Singing Love Pen* and about 100 yards from the east end of the ledge system at

Climbers on Valentine's Day (5.8+). MAREA ROSS PHOTO

Moderate Mecca
Left

To
1st
Pullout

a varnished, left-facing corner. Carry gear up to a #3.5 Friend. Stem up the nice corner to a ledge. There are 2 belay bolts just to the left of the top of the route.

**9    Ace of Hearts (5.10+ TR)** It appears this route was aided with thin pitons (hence the route name) prior to being free-climbed. Start 20' left of the *Valentine's Day* corner below a varnished face. Climb up along thin, vertical cracks to the top. This can be toproped after doing *Valentine's Day*.

There is a large yellow recess 200' left of the last route. The ledge system traversing the cliff crosses a talus slope at this point.

**10    Pending Disaster (5.9+)** This is one of the better routes on the crag. Bring a full rack up to a #4 Camalot. Rope up at the right edge of a large yellow recess below an obvious crack system. Jam a left-slanting crack past a low overhang. Continue up obvious, steep cracks to a lower-angled face. Rappel with one rope from the belay anchor.

**11    Penny Lane (5.3)** About 200 yards from the right (east) edge of the cliff is a large recess with a huge corner in the back. Romp up the huge, left-facing corner system to the summit. Watch out for loose rocks. Walk off right (east). (No topo.)

**12    Abbey Road (5.4)** Bring wires, TCUs, and some long slings. Begin 10' left of the last route (the huge corner) and 75' left of *Pending Disaster* at prominent thin cracks on a slabby face. Face-climb up along the thin cracks to a small alcove. Pull over a small ceiling, then climb up another 10' to a ledge. Either

*Climber on Scalawag (5.10). MAREA ROSS PHOTO*

continue to the top of the cliff or traverse 40' left to an anchor. You need two ropes for the rappel from the anchor. If you go to the top, walk off right (east).

**13    Fleet Street (5.8 PG)** If you are fleet-footed, this route won't seem bad. Carry some small wires to supplement the 2 bolts on this route. Climb the center of the black, varnished face just left of the last route. Belay and rappel from the communal anchor on a ledge about 100' up.

**14    Muckraker (5.8)** Carry gear up to a #3 Friend. Start 25' left of the last route at the right-hand of two cracks leading through a roof. Climb the crack past the right side of the roof (crux), then up the lower-angled wide crack to its top. Angle up and left to the communal belay. Rappel with two ropes.

**15    Scalawag (5.10)** A wild route that protects well with multiple large cams. Rope up at the left-hand of two roof cracks in an alcove. Traverse out the crack to a stance, then up past the lip to lower-angle terrain. Finish up a crack system that forms an X. Rappel with two ropes from the communal anchor.

**16    Boodler (5.8+ PG)** An interesting and challenging route for the solid leader. Start 40' left (west) of *Scalawag* and around a nose of rock. The route climbs the left-leaning ramp/corner to an anchor about 60' up. Bring small wires, lots of small TCUs, and cams to #3.5.

**17    Carpetbagger (5.6+)** Rope up 70' left of the last route at a huge openbook. Climb the large corner system to an anchor on a ledge. Carry gear to a #3 cam. Rappel with one rope.

**18    The Haj (5.9)** A good route. Begin 30' left of *Carpetbagger* on the left side of a pink overhang. The route starts near an acacia bush and below a varnished, left-facing corner. Jam and stem up the steep corner to lower-angle terrain. Carry gear up to a #3 cam. Rappel from the communal anchor with one rope. (No topo.)

**19    Sir Climbalot (5.7 PG)** Begin in the same place as the last route on the left edge of a pink overhang (near an acacia bush on the traverse ledge). Climb the low-angle, left-facing corner that is just left of a steep, varnished corner. The crux is near the bottom, pulling a bulge (#1.5 Friend or Tri-Cam in a pocket). Bring gear to a #3 cam and rappel from the communal anchor with one rope. Watch for loose rock near the anchor. (No topo.)

**20    The Route to Mecca (5.7)** A pretty good route for the grade. Rope up 10' left of the last route at a short, pink, left-facing corner. This is just left of an acacia (cat's claw) bush. Bring gear to a #2.5 Friend. Climb the corner, then pull past a bulge at a varnished crack (crux). Continue up the low-angle, left-facing corner to its top. Wander up past several ledges (watch for loose rock) to a communal anchor. Rappel with one rope.

The next cliffs described are all on the north-facing hillside several hundred yards to the right of the picnic area. For the best approach, follow the well-worn path leading northwest along the base of the hillside from the Red Spring Picnic Area. The crags are described from left to right as viewed from the trail.

## Cannibal Crag

This huge boulder is about 300 yards to the northwest of Red Spring Picnic Area and just above the well-defined trail that contours along the hillside. The boulder is in the sun for a good part of the day and harbors some excellent climbs. Climbs are described from left to right starting on the extreme left end of the formation. As you approach the cliff along the trail, you arrive on the southeast face near *Caustic*. The first four climbs described are on the overhanging south wall and face away from the trail.

**21    Maneater (5.12a)** Start just right of the easy descent route on the back of the formation. Four bolts lead to a cold-shut anchor.

**22    Wonderstuff (5.12d)** Rope up 8' right of the last route below the leftmost line of 6 bolts. There is an obvious hole in the rock between the second and third

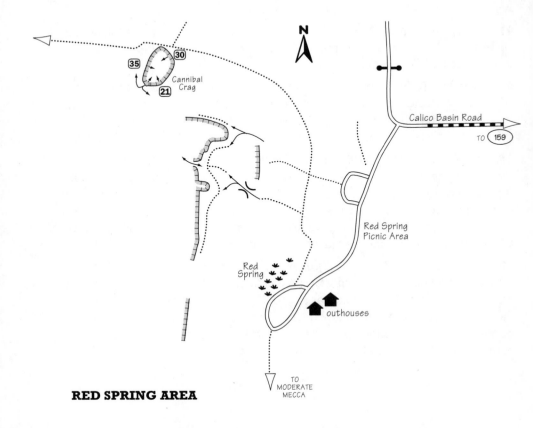

**RED SPRING AREA**

bolts. It seems like most people are now avoiding the first bolt by traversing in from the left. If you start from the very bottom of the route, bring a #1 or #1.5 TCU to get to the first bolt (or stick-clip). (Not shown.)

**23   New Wave Hookers (5.12c)** Rope up as for the last route just above a pit. Power past 6 bolts heading right, then up past honeycombed rock.

**24   Fear this Sport (5.12b)** Start 12' downhill of the last two routes. Angle out right toward the arête, passing 5 bolts.

The next routes are on the eastern side of the formation and are visible from the trail. There may or may not be anchors on top.

**25   Caliban (5.8+ PG)** A bit contrived near the bottom, but an OK route nonetheless. Begin 20' left of the obvious left-leaning crack at a hole in the rock. Climb the low-angle face past 3 bolts to cold shuts. The 5.8+ (and most obvious) route moves right past the first bolt, then way back left to the second bolt (hence the PG rating).

**26   You Are What You Eat (5.3)** Climb the obvious left-leaning crack.

**27   Baseboy (5.10d PG)** Rope up at the base of a *You Are What You Eat*, the obvious left-leaning crack. Jam up the crack for 20', clip 2 bolts, and move right and up past 1 more bolt. Lower off the fourth bolt or go to the top.

**28    Save the Heart to Eat Later (5.12a)** Begin 40' left of the arête and just left of some Native American petroglyphs (do not touch!). Angle up left past 3 bolts before lowering off.

**29    Pickled (5.11c)** Same start as the last route. Shoot up a slabby face to a bolt, then angle up right past 4 bolts. It's common to lower off the last bolt.

**30    Caustic (5.11b PG)** This good route climbs the arête separating the east and west faces directly above the well-worn trail that contours along the hillside. Start to the right of the arête and climb easy rock out left (a bit scary; possible TCU placement before reaching the arête) onto the edge. Or, climb straight up the arête utilizing a bolt down low that was recently added. Most people lower off the fourth bolt.

The next routes (not pictured) are on the varnished west face of the formation. Because the majority of these shady routes are moderate in nature, this face is quite popular.

**31    Have a Beer with Fear (5.11a)** Begin at the left edge of the wall. Climb past 4 bolts, either lowering off the last bolt or going to the summit. The height-related crux is by the first bolt.

**32    Fear This (5.11+)** Start 8' right of the last route. Follow 3 bolts to cold shuts.

**33    Elbows of Mac and Ronnie (5.10d)** Begin 10' right of the last route at a right-leaning flake/ramp. Climb up and right past 4 bolts to the cold-shut anchor.

**34    What's Eating You? (5.9+)** Start 10' left of *Elbows of Mac and Ronnie* at a left-facing flake leading to a bulge. Saunter past 3 bolts to the top, where you need TCUs or Friends for the anchor.

**35    A Man in Every Pot (5.8+)** Begin 8' right of the last route at the left edge of the white boulder leaning against the crag. Scamper up the face past 3 bolts to the top. Bring a couple of TCUs for pro and the anchor.

**36    Mac and Ronnie in Cheese (5.10-)** Begin 3' right of the right edge of a white boulder leaning against the west face of the cliff. Climb to a bolt about 8' up (added recently), then continue straight up past 2 more bolts to the top. You may want to bring a few TCUs for the climb and the belay. Walk off right (southwest).

**37    Ma and Pa in Kettle (5.7-)** Start at a varnished, left-facing corner that is at the very right edge of the face and 20' right of a white boulder leaning against the cliff. There are 3 bolts for protection on the face above the corner, and TCUs make up the belay. Walk off right.

**38    Shishka Bob (5.6 X)** Climb the very short, varnished face on the upper right side of the wall.

# FIRST PULLOUT AREA OVERVIEW

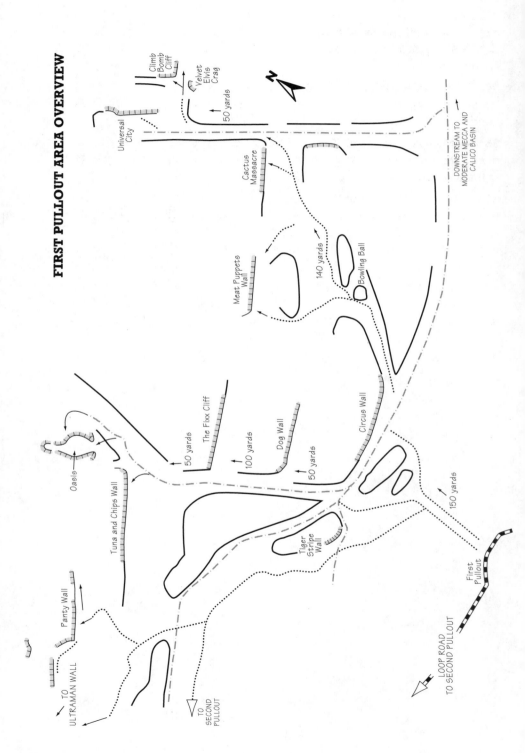

Climb Bomb Cliff

Velvet Elvis Crag

Universal City

50 yards

Cactus Massacre

Meat Puppets Wall

140 yards

Bowling Ball

DOWNSTREAM TO MODERATE MECCA AND CALICO BASIN

N

The Fixx Cliff

Oasis

50 yards

Tuna and Chips Wall

Dog Wall

100 yards

50 yards

Circus Wall

150 yards

Panty Wall

Tiger Stripe Wall

TO ULTRAMAN WALL

TO SECOND PULLOUT

First Pullout

LOOP ROAD TO SECOND PULLOUT

## CHAPTER TWO

# First Pullout

Three crags are described in this chapter, probably the best of which are Dog Wall and The Fixx Cliff. The Fixx Cliff was one of the first small, modern cliffs to be developed at Red Rocks and subsequently led to establishing popular cliffs like The Gallery. All of these routes have very short approaches and generally are in the sun most of the day. To reach First Pullout, drive the scenic loop road for 1.1 miles and park in the designated area on the right.

## Dog Wall

A popular sport cliff with a quick approach. Walk down the trail from the parking lot to the wash, then go left 200 feet to the edge of Circus Wall. The Dog Wall is

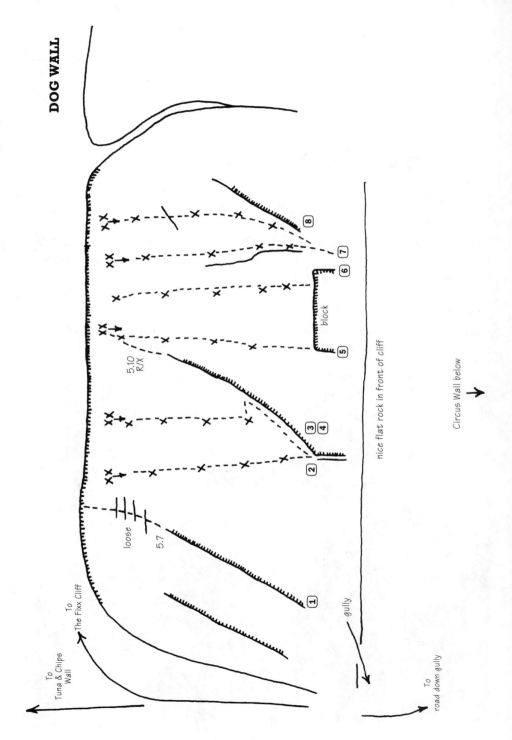

about 150 feet up a gully to the right on the next level above Circus Wall. This cliff is plainly visible from the trailhead, appearing as the lowest good face. Routes are described from left to right. To access the top, continue up the gully about 50 feet, then go right. From the top of the routes, walk off left.

**1      Wok the Dog (5.7)** Bring your pooper-scooper. Near the left edge of the crag and above the approach gully, climb a low-angle, right-leaning ramp to the top of the wall.

**2      Cat Walk (5.10a)** Begin 40' right at the left end of a right-leaning ramp/ flake and about 75' up from the drainage. Climb past 4 bolts to a chain anchor.

**3      It's a Bitch (5.10b)** Start 5' right of *Cat Walk* and crank past 4 bolts to a cold-shut anchor.

**4      Man's Best Friend (5.10 R/X)** Not exactly. Climb the right-leaning ramp/flake noted in the last two routes and finish up the unprotected face.

**5      Here Kitty, Kitty (5.11c)** Begin 30' right of the ramp/flake, atop a block. Power past 4 bolts to a cold-shut anchor. Rebolted in 1991 after having been chopped long ago.

**6      K-9 (5.12b)** Gear up 8' right of the last route at the right end of a block at the base of the cliff. Climb past 5 bolts to the bolt anchor on top.

**7      Cujo (5.11d)** Rope up 5' right at a white streak and just left of a large flake. Climb past 5 bolts to a cold-shut anchor.

First Pullout

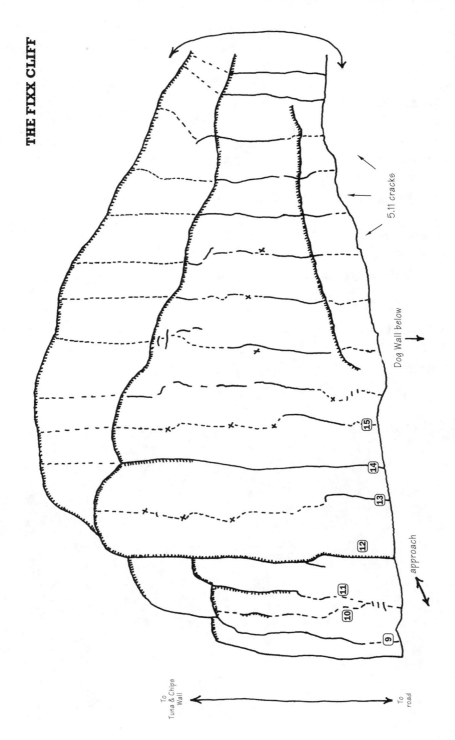

THE FIXX CLIFF

5.11 cracks

Dog Wall below

approach

To Tuna & Chips Wall

To road

**8    Poodle Chainsaw Massacre (5.11c)**  Start at a right-leaning flake 5' right of the last route. Climb past 4 bolts to a cold-shut anchor.

## The Fixx Cliff

The first semi-sport cliff to be developed in the area. Bring traditional gear for the routes here. Follow the trail from the parking lot down to the wash, then turn left (northwest) and follow the drainage about 200 feet until it turns uphill. About 250 feet up from the bottom of the wash (and 100 feet above the turnoff for Dog Wall) the drainage is split by a rock shaped like the prow of a ship. Take the right fork (straight ahead) and scramble up about 300 feet. The cliff is on your right. Like Dog Wall, this cliff is plainly visible from the trailhead, level with the road, and just left of center as you view the cliff bands. Routes are described from left to right. Descend off the right side.

**9    The Whiff (5.10- PG)**  This finger-and-hand crack is near the left edge of the cliff. The climb is a bit hard to protect.

**10    Snow Blind (5.11 R)**  Start 10' right of *The Whiff* and climb steep huecos past 1 bolt to a vague arête.

**11    Stand or Fall (5.11-)**  Begin 5' right of the last route and climb steep huecos past 1 bolt to a crack.

**12    Crack (5.11)**  Crank up the obvious finger crack 8' right of the last route.

**13    Free Base (5.11)**  Rope up 10' right of *Crack* and climb a vertical crack to 3 bolts along an overhanging seam. Good climbing on this one.

**14    Saved by Zero (5.11)**  Climb the classic steep finger-and-hand crack that is 10' right of *Free Base*.

**15    Red Skies (5.11+)**  Follow a seam and 3 bolts 5' right of *Saved by Zero*.

Note: The cracks to the right are about 5.11.

## Tuna and Chips Wall

Follow the trail from the parking lot down to the wash, then turn left (northwest) and follow the drainage about 200 feet until it turns uphill. About 250 feet up from the bottom of the wash (and 100 feet above the turnoff for Dog Wall), the drainage is split by a rock shaped like the prow of a ship. Take the right fork (straight ahead) and scramble up about 300 feet. The Fixx Cliff will be on your right. Continue up the drainage past the Fixx Cliff about 150 feet to a big, plated cliff blocking the drainage. You will arrive at the center of the cliff, just right of a low-angled crack and directly below a water streak. Routes on this sunny cliff are described from right to left. Walk off to the right (east) and then follow a gully back to the base of the cliff.

**16    Chips Ahoy! (5.9 R)** Start 50' right of the crack/gully in the center of the cliff and atop boulders below left-slanting seams. **Pitch 1 (5.8 R)**: Climb steep varnished rock above the left-slanting seams and continue up the plated face above, passing 2 bolts to a 2-bolt belay. 120'. **Pitch 2 (5.9)**: Power through the roof above (bolt, crux) to easier ground and the top of the formation. 100'. Descend off right.

**17    Tuna Cookies (5.7 R)** If you've seen the movie *Traxx*, this route name will make sense. Begin just left of the last route, at several left-arching seams. Bring wires and gear to a #3 Friend. **Pitch 1 (5.7 R)**: Climb up left to a bolt 30' up, then continue up the center of the long face past 1 more bolt to the ceiling. Climb past the left edge to a big ledge. 150'. **Pitch 2 (5.2)**: Scramble to the top. 100'. Descend off right.

**18    Waterstreak (5.8 PG)** The difficulty is dependent on exactly where you climb. Going directly up the streak could be as hard as 5.10. Gear up 30' left of the last route at the base of an obvious water streak, which is 20' right of a low-angle crack. Climb past 3 bolts to join the main crack/chimney system (bolt and drilled piton in the alcove). Rappel, or continue up the crack to the top.

**19    Chips and Salsa (5.3)** Rope up at the base of the central crack/chimney system and directly behind a block. Follow the crack for about 200' to the top. Descend off right.

**20    Tuna and Chips (5.7 R)** Start 20' left of the central crack at the left edge of a block. Bring up to a #2 Friend. **Pitch 1 (5.7 R)**: Climb a low-angle face, keeping right of a black, left-facing flake. Follow 3 bolts to a belay in a vertical crack (small gear needed). 150'. **Pitch 2 (5.3)**: Continue up the crack and face to the top. 60'. Descend off right.

# CHAPTER THREE

# Second Pullout

This area has some of the best sport climbing cliffs at Red Rocks. The Gallery, Wall of Confusion, and Black Corridor are of excellent quality and extremely popular. They are so popular, in fact, that the disposal of human waste and other environmental issues are of great concern to land managers. Please do your part to reduce impacts, not only here but at every climbing area you visit!

Park at Second Pullout, 1.7 miles from the start of the scenic loop road, to approach any of these crags. The cliffs at this pullout are described from right to left (from the direction of First Pullout, moving left toward the Sandstone Quarry).

## *Magic Bus*

This small crag hosts a number of moderate routes and has become a popular cold-weather spot for intermediate climbers. It is visible directly to the north of Second Pullout about halfway up the rocky hillside. The crag is an obvious black block with a small, red triangle near its lower right corner. There are several dark, angular boulders at the top of the ridge just above this wall.

From Second Pullout, follow the main trail down to the wash level. Cross the wash and walk straight north toward the red outcrop. Follow a hidden gully with a smooth south wall up and right (east) for 250 feet to a fault. Scramble up left (north) along the fault/gully for 75 feet to an open, relatively flat area. The formation is located about 150 feet up and right (northeast) from this point. Routes are described from left to right as you approach. The approach takes about 15 minutes. (No topo.)

**1    Electric Koolaid (5.9+)** The loose face just right of the formation's left edge has been lead. Belay from the anchors on *Blonde Dwarf.* (Not shown.)

**2    Blonde Dwarf (5.10-)** The obvious thin crack that curves right and up. When the crack ends, follow 2 bolts up left on steep rock to a cold-shut anchor. Bring a good selection of small to medium protection for the crack.

**3    Neon Sunset (5.8)** Climb the center of the wall past 9 bolts with red hangers to a chain anchor. This route is 15' right of *Blonde Dwarf* and is very well protected (some might say overbolted). (Not shown.)

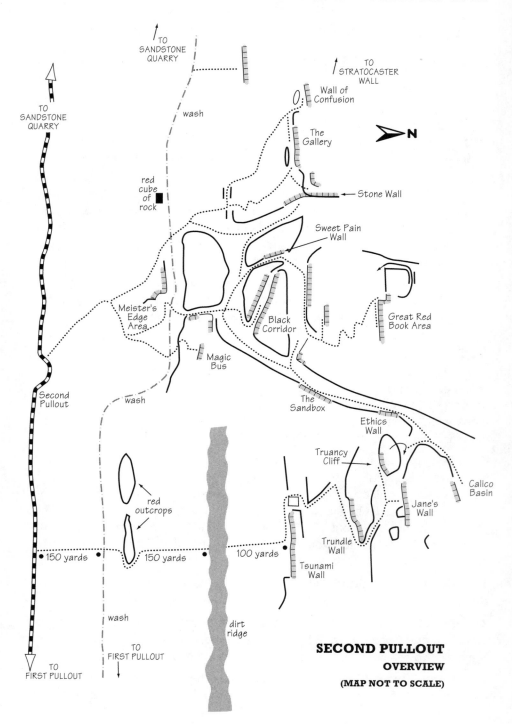

TO
SANDSTONE
QUARRY

TO
STRATOCASTER
WALL

Wall of
Confusion

The
Gallery

N

wash

TO
SANDSTONE
QUARRY

Stone Wall

red
cube
of
rock

Sweet Pain
Wall

Meister's
Edge
Area

Black
Corridor

Great Red
Book Area

Magic
Bus

Second
Pullout

wash

The
Sandbox

Ethics
Wall

Truancy
Cliff

Calico
Basin

red
outcrops

Jane's
Wall

•150 yards •   •150 yards   •   100 yards •

Trundle
Wall

Tsunami
Wall

wash

TO
FIRST PULLOUT

dirt
ridge

**SECOND PULLOUT**
**OVERVIEW**
**(MAP NOT TO SCALE)**

TO
FIRST PULLOUT

**4     Zipperhead (5.8 PG13)** Rope up 8' right of *Neon Sunset* at a thin, vertical crack in varnished rock. Follow the crack for 20', then step right and go up another seam to a bolt. Angle either left or right to reach an anchor on one of the adjoining routes. Bring gear to a #1 Friend. (Not shown.)

**5     Technicolor Sunrise (5.8 PG)** Begin 6' right of the last line at the left edge of a smooth, triangular section of rock. Climb the left edge of the triangle, then straight up the face past 4 bolts to 2 cold shuts. Small wires are helpful near the bottom of the route.

**6     Ken Queasy (5.8 PG13)** Start 12' right of the last climb and 8' left of the cliff's edge. Climb a thin, vertical seam in steep, black rock to a bolt, then straight up to another bolt. Angle up left to join *Technicolor Sunrise* from its last bolt. A small TCU and RPs will help you reach the first bolt. (Not shown.)

## *The Black Corridor*

This corridor, which runs southeast-northwest, currently hosts a total of 25 routes on both walls. The climbs are generally of a moderate nature, making this a popular destination. For an added challenge, try to do all of the routes in a day! This is also a good place to experience the true meaning of generic sport climbs. We can only hope this sort of development won't be repeated in too many other places. The approach is quite simple, although the corridor or its entrance can't be seen from the parking lot. Follow the trail down from Second Pullout and take the second left (the first goes to The Gallery/Wall of Confusion).

Follow this trail across a red sandy area, then turn slightly right into a drainage (the main wash curves left/west toward The Gallery). Scramble over rocks for 100 yards (you may have to avoid water) to an open area.

Continue north for 50 yards until your progress is blocked by a bush-filled corridor. Traverse 75 feet right (east) on a ledge system just above the bushes, then curve left toward trees at the entrance of the corridor. This sounds complicated, but once you've done it, the whole approach takes less than 10 minutes. These climbs are in the shade most of the time and are described from the lower entrance moving up the corridor. All routes have anchors on top. (No topos.)

### Left/South Wall, Lower Level

**7      Bonaire (5.9)**  Start 75' in from the lower corridor entrance. Climb past 6 bolts with homemade hangers to an anchor. The first bolt is stupid.

**8      Bon Ez (5.9+)**  Begin 20' right of the last route and climb past 7 bolts to an anchor. Again, the first bolt isn't needed.

**9      Crude Boys (5.10d)**  Rope up 15' right of the last route, then clip 6 bolts en route to an anchor on top. There is an overhang in the middle of the route.

**10     Black Corridor Route 4 Left (5.11a)**  This route shares the anchor with the last route. Deceptively difficult. Start 8' right of *Crude Boys* and climb the slippery rock past 2 bolts to a horizontal crack. Move left and finish on *Crude Boys*.

**11     BCR 5L (5.10+)**  Begin 10' right of the last route and 20' left of the boulders that divide the corridor into two levels. Climb past 1 bolt to a thin, vertical crack and follow it to the top.

**12     Vagabonds (5.10a)**  Climb the groove and face 6' right of the last route, clipping 8 bolts on your way to the anchor.

**13     Crude Control (5.12a)**  Contrived and difficult at the start. Begin 12' right of *Vagabonds* and just left of the boulders that divide the corridor into two levels. Follow 6 bolts to the anchor.

### Right/North Wall, Basement

**14     Adoption (5.11b)**  Stiff climbing right off the ground. Start at the entrance to the corridor and climb the plated face past 6 bolts.

**15     Burros Don't Gamble (5.10c)**  Begin near a tree about 20' left of *Adoption*. Climb a huecoed face to a flake, then on to the top, passing 7 bolts to a shared anchor.

**16     Burros Might Fly (5.10a R)**  Start about 30' left of *Adoption* and 10' left of the last route. Climb a right-leaning ramp to a bolt. Go straight up on thin edges to a flake. Make a long runout across a flake to the fourth bolt, then on up to the shared anchor.

**17   Nightmare on Crude Street (5.10d)**   A little loose, but that gives it some character! This route is directly across from *Bonaire* (the route with homemade hangers) and climbs overhanging, red rock past 5 bolts to an anchor. Climbing directly between each bolt makes the climb about 5.11b and contrived.

### Left Wall, Upper Level

**18   Thermal Breakdown (5.9+ PG)**   Begin atop the dividing boulders and cruise past some big ledges and 6 bolts.

**19   Crude Street Blues (5.9+ PG)**   Start at a stupidly placed bolt 15' right of the last route. Climb past ledges and 4 bolts to the anchor.

**20   Crude Behavior (5.9+)**   Rope up at a ramp 8' right of *Crude Street Blues*. Scamper past 4 bolts to an anchor.

**21   Dancin' with a God (5.10a)**   One of the better routes in its grade. Start 12' right of the last route and 35' right of the dividing boulders. Follow 6 bolts to an anchor.

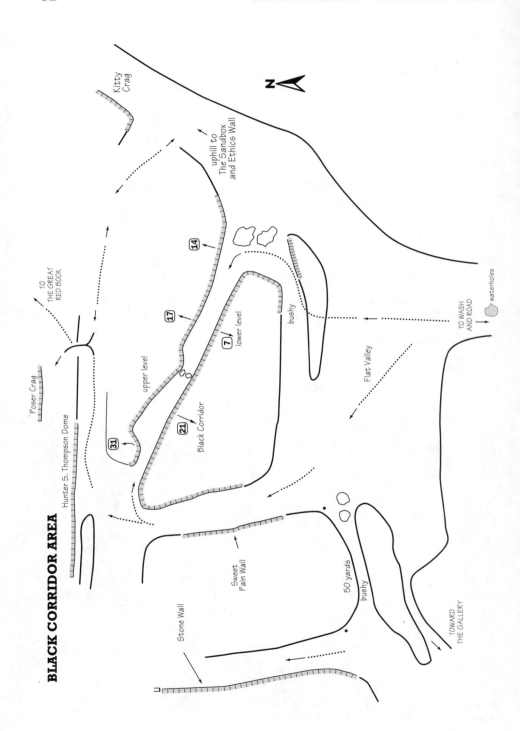

BLACK CORRIDOR AREA

Kitty Crag

uphill to
The Sandbox
and Ethics Wall

N

TO
THE GREAT
RED BOOK

14

17

7    lower level

upper level

bushy

31

21

Black Corridor

Poser Crag

Hunter S. Thompson Dome

Flat Valley

waterholes

TO WASH
AND ROAD

Sweet
Pain Wall

Stone Wall

50 yards

bushy

TOWARD
THE GALLERY

**22    Live Fast, Die Young (5.10d)** This one may be harder for tall folks. Start 8' right of *Dancin' with a God*. Follow 5 bolts to the anchor—if you can do the mantle at the start.

**23    Black Gold (5.10b)** Begin at a small flake 6' to the right of the last route. Follow 5 bolts with hangers to chains.

**24    Texas Tea (5.10a)** From the route names, you can tell these guys watched *The Beverly Hillbillies*! Start at the left edge of a large flake 8' right of the last route. Climb the smooth face to a small ceiling (bolt), then up past 4 more to an anchor. The crux is at the bottom and is contrived.

**25    Fool's Gold (5.10b)** A broken hold has made this climb harder. Same start as the last route, but walk up right on a ramp. Face-climb past numerous huecos and 5 bolts to an anchor.

### Right Wall, Second Story

**26    Oils Well that Ends Well (5.11a)** Start about 10' left of the dividing boulders and just left of a right-leaning crack system. Climb past 5 bolts (if you get past the second, you should be home free) to the anchor.

**27    Sandstone Enema (5.11b)** Begin 10' left of the last route, below a short, right-leaning ramp and 10' right of a sentry box. Tricky moves past the first 2 bolts lead to easier climbing past 4 more on the slabby face above. If you start on the left and climb by the hangerless bolt, the route is 5.10d/.11a.

**28    Lewd, Crude, and Misconstrued (5.9+ PG)** One of the longer routes in the corridor. Start at a sentry box/left-facing corner that is 10' left of *Sandstone Enema* and just left of a boulder in the corridor. Power up the corner and arête past 6 bolts to the anchor.

**29    Texas Lite Sweet (5.11b PG)** Rope up 6' left of the last route and climb past 3 bolts with hangers to a chain anchor under a ceiling.

**30    Livin' on Borrowed Time (5.11c)** Begin 3' left of the last route at smooth, varnished rock with a crescent-shaped hold by the first bolt. Follow 4 bolts to the anchor.

**31    Rebel without a Pause (5.11a)** Probably the best route here. Climb the overhanging huecos 50' left of the last route and just right of the upper entrance to Black Corridor. Follow 4 bolts to a chain anchor.

## The Gallery

This is the most popular sport climbing cliff at Red Rocks and probably the best place to meet climbers. Human waste is a *big* problem here! Do your part: pack it out, and chastise those who don't.

From the parking area, walk down the main trail, then take the first trail leading off to the left (about 120 yards from the lot). Follow this lesser-used trail about 400 yards up over a red outcrop (the top of the Meister's Edge Area), then down to a wash and pine tree. Cross the wash immediately (well before another pine and a large, red cube of rock) and follow a well-trodden path up broken slabs for 100 yards to a small corridor running parallel to the hillside. Either scramble up the far wall of the corridor (about 30' of scrambling) and then angle up left across slabs for 75 yards to the base of the wall, or go left in the gully, then walk up slabs.

You should arrive at the right (east) end of the crag under the most overhanging section of rock if you did the scrambling, and at the left (west) end if you took the easy way. This approach takes about 15 minutes. The cliff is visible from the road (although it looks very small and insignificant) and is in the sun most of the day. Routes are described from right to left. All routes have anchors from which to grab, lower, rappel, or toprope. (See photo for Second Pullout, page 31.)

**32    Glitch (5.12c)** Start 10' left of an alcove on the right side of The Gallery. Follow a right-leaning flake past 4 bolts, then continue up right past a hueco and 2 more bolts to the anchor.

**33    Nothing Shocking (5.13a)** Climb *Glitch* to the third bolt, then power straight up past 3 more bolts to join the end of *The Sissy Traverse*.

**34    Who Made Who (5.12c)** Climb *Glitch* to the second bolt, then continue up past 3 more bolts.

**35    Where the Down Boys Go (5.12d)** Start at the bottom of the flake that the last three routes climb and go up and slightly left past 5 bolts.

**36    The Gift (5.12d)** Start at the base of *Yaak Crack* and climb up very steep rock past 6 bolts.

**37    Yaak Crack (5.11d)** Begin 8' left of the last four routes and below the obvious left-leaning crack. Climb the crack past 6 bolts.

**38    The Sissy Traverse (5.13b)** Start in the corridor behind the right edge of a huge boulder that is 15' left of *Yaak Crack*. The bolts on this route have been painted black so that you know you're on the right route! Climb up to the first bolt (see variation), then angle right and up past 8 more bolts. **Variation:** Start at the base of *Yaak Crack* and climb past the first 3 bolts on *The Gift* before going up right past 5 more bolts. This seems to be the more logical line.

**39    Minstrel in the Gallery (5.12b)** The first route on the cliff. Same start as *The Sissy Traverse,* then climb the face just left of *Yaak Crack* past 5 bolts.

**40    A Day in the Life (5.11b)** Begin 10' left of the last route, behind the huge boulder and on the left side of a cat's claw bush. Cruise out the right side of the pod past 5 bolts.

**41    Social Disorder (5.11d)** Rope up as for the last route, then climb straight up from the pod past 5 bolts.

**42    Gridlock (5.11c)** Same start as the past two routes but exit out the left side of the pod, passing 4 bolts with homemade hangers. It's a little easier to go left, then back right between the second and third bolts.

**43    Running Amuck (5.10c)** Rope up 10' left of the last route below a short, left-facing flake and up on a ledge. Run past 4 bolts to the same anchor as *Gridlock.*

**44    Pump First, Pay Later (5.10b)** Don't run out of gas before you get to the anchor! Start 6' left of the last route, clipping 4 bolts.

**45    Gelatin Pooch (5.10a)** Begin 6' left and climb past 4 bolts (3 have homemade hangers) to chains.

**46    Buck's Muscle World (5.9-)** Start 8' left of *Gelatin Pooch* to climb this 3-bolt route with homemade hangers.

**47    Sport Climbing Is Neither (5.8)** Start 10' left of *Buck's Muscle World* at a short, curving crack. Follow 3 bolts to an anchor.

**48    Range of Motion (5.10d)** Start about 75' left of *Buck's Muscle World* and 20' left of a right-facing corner that doesn't reach the ground. Climb up through a pod, passing 4 bolts.

## *Wall of Confusion*

This cliff is about 150' left of The Gallery on the same level. Routes are described from right to left because the normal approach is from The Gallery. All routes have anchors. Believe it or not, these routes were done before The Gallery was developed.

**49    Body English (5.12c)** Start 30' up and right from *Fear and Loathing III* at the very right end of the cliff. Climb the steep corner past 4 bolts to chains (or go left to the anchor on *Fear and Loathing III*).

**50    Fear and Loathing III (5.12a)** One of the steepest routes you've seen until you go to *The Trophy.* This is at least the third *Fear and Loathing* at Red Rocks. Start atop a boulder in an alcove and power past several roofs on an overhanging wall. There are 9 bolts providing convenient places to hang and rest.

**51    Promises in the Dark (5.12b)** Begin 12' left of the last route at a short dihedral capped by a ceiling. Zip past 7 bolts to the anchor.

**52    Big Damage (5.12b)** Start at a right-curving crack 6' left of *Promises in the Dark* and climb up and slightly left past 6 bolts.

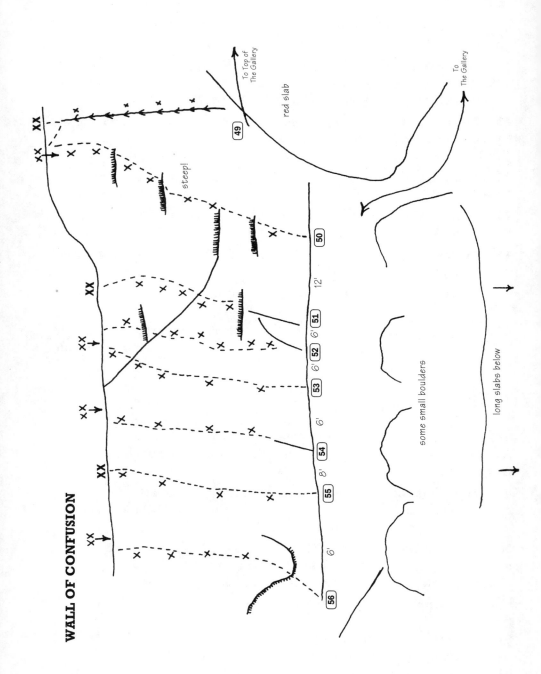

**WALL OF CONFUSION**

**53**   **Sudden Impact (5.11c)**  Climb the face 6' (see topo) left of the last route, passing 5 bolts.

**54**   **Desert Pickle (5.11b)**  Power up the wall 6' left of the last route, using 4 bolts.

**55**   **American Sportsman (5.10c)**  Another 4-bolt route 8' (see topo) left of the last route.

**56**   **The Runaway (5.10b PG)**  The farthest left route on the cliff. It starts up on a ledge. There are 4 bolts with homemade hangers for pro.

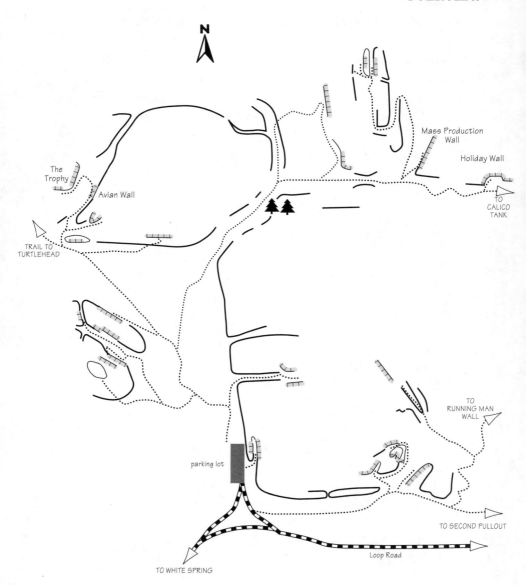

N

The Trophy

Avian Wall

TRAIL TO TURTLEHEAD

Mass Production Wall

Holiday Wall

TO CALICO TANK

TO RUNNING MAN WALL

parking lot

TO SECOND PULLOUT

Loop Road

TO WHITE SPRING

CHAPTER FOUR

# Sandstone Quarry

This area has a host of worthwhile 1-pitch crags containing climbs of all difficulties. The approaches range from 1 to 25 minutes. Follow the scenic loop road for 2.7 miles and park in the large lot at Sandstone Quarry. The first routes described are to the right (southeast) of the parking lot (toward the Second Pullout).

## Running Man Wall Area

This collection of sunny cliffs is located to the southeast of the parking lot and back toward Second Pullout. From the southeast corner of the Sandstone Quarry parking lot, walk along a trail back toward Second Pullout, aiming for the outermost section of exposed white rock (about 200 yards).

Continue east on this trail along the right (south) slope of a small canyon, then drop down left (north) between two red outcrops to the bottom of the drainage. You pass a large, mushroom-shaped boulder just before reaching the drainage bottom. Walk 50 yards down the drainage, passing two pine trees, then veer left (north and east) and scramble 100 yards up red slabs to a huge terrace with a large, black block above. This black block is the *Boschton Marathon Block.*

### Boschton Marathon Block
1    **Boschton Marathon (5.12b)**  This route is located on the front of the large, black block. It is clearly visible from the loop road, has 6 bolts, and is slightly tricky to downclimb from the summit.

2    **Frictiony Face, Panty Waist (5.8+)**  This popular route is located just right of *Boschton Marathon,* on a red slab. Start 20' up above the huge terrace on a ledge that is just right of the huge black block and behind a large cat's claw (acacia) bush. The route has 6 bolts and ends at a 2-bolt belay station 85' up.

### Running Man Wall
From the Boschton Marathon Block, angle right (east) on the terrace for 125 yards to Running Man Wall, which faces the loop road (south). A long, low roof running along the majority of the crag characterizes it.

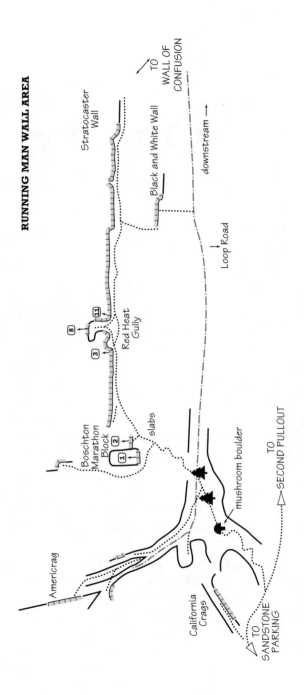

RUNNING MAN WALL AREA

Routes are described from left to right, and the routes in this guide are near the right edge of the formation. You will need two ropes to get off most routes. (Not all routes appear in photo on page 42.)

**3      Running Man (5.11)** Definitely better than the movie! One of the classic pitches at Red Rocks. Start below an obvious vertical seam system that trends slightly up and left. Use your Schwarzenegger-like muscles to power past lots of bolts to a bolt anchor. You may want to bring a few TCUs and small wires to supplement the bolts.

**4      Graveyard Waltz (5.11d PG)** Rather sporty, but great climbing. Same start as *Running Man,* but climb just to the right, going straight up past 9 bolts with homemade hangers.

**5      Commando (5.12b)** Begin at the left edge of a low ceiling that is just left of a right-facing corner 10' right of the last route. Follow 9 bolts that lead to an anchor. At press time, there was an unfinished route just right of this.

**6      Galloping Gal (5.11a)** Being tall helps on this one. Rope up 45' right of the last route and 3' left of a left-facing chimney/corner. Starting atop a pink pedestal, climb past 10 bolts to a chain anchor 85' up.

**7      Vile Pile (5.10 PG)** Bring #1.5 and #2 Friends to place between the fourth and fifth bolts. Start 5' right of *Galloping Gal* and 10' left of an oak bush atop a pink pedestal. Zip past 6 bolts to the top of the block. Rap from an anchor.

Right of the *Vile Pile* formation is a gully leading up into a recess. The next routes are in this gully.

**8      Red Heat (5.10+ PG 13)** Another excellent route. Scramble 100' up the obvious gully, to the right of *Vile Pile,* to ledges. Climb a right-facing, varnished groove past 5 bolts, then continue up the face past 4 more bolts to an anchor in a hueco. Bring some cams and plan on a two-rope rappel.

**9      Synthetic Society (5.11a)** A bit contrived. Scramble up the *Red Heat* gully for 40'. On the right (east) wall of the gully, climb past the left edge of a ceiling and 7 bolts to a chain anchor shared with *Plastic People.*

**10    Plastic People (5.10b)** Same start as the last route, 40' up the *Red Heat* gully. Trend out right to the arête, then up to the shared chain anchor, clipping 8 bolts en route.

**11    Fibonacci Wall (5.11+)** If you're not a math major, you'll need to look this one up in the dictionary. The name should go with a 5.8 climb. Climb the rounded arête on the right edge of the *Red Heat* gully past 7 bolts.

# Sandstone Quarry North

## *Avian Wall*

These shady routes are located on a north-facing wall just below The Trophy. They all are on primarily white rock and have anchors from which to lower. To get there, walk 200 yards northwest from the parking lot on the main trail, past a white boulder in the main wash, to an old roadway. Follow the roadway for about another 200 yards to an obvious oak bush on the left side of the trail. Turn left off the roadway onto the trail that goes to Turtlehead. After about 200 yards, this footpath goes up over a dirt hump. Follow the trail along the top of the dirt mound until you reach white rocks. At this point, Turtlehead Trail turns right and goes down into the wash. Continue on the trail, which goes diagonally across the wash/valley toward white rocks and Turtlehead itself. The first white formation that the trail reaches is The Twinkie. Walk just past The Twinkie, then turn right off the trail toward a smooth, brown wave of rock (The Drive-In). Go northeast up the canyon about 100 yards to the cliff, which makes up the right (east) wall of the canyon. The Trophy (described next) is 200 feet up slabs to the left. Routes are described from right to left as you head up the gully. Approach time is about 15 minutes. (No topo.)

**12    Spotted Owl (5.11a)**  No redwoods here! Start 20' right of a large oak tree at a flat sandy spot. Climb up along vertical seams, clipping 5 bolts before you reach the chain anchor.

**13    Thunderbird (5.11b PG)**  Not your typical crimper. This one requires a bit of technique. Begin in a pit 80' left of the last route and follow 6 bolts along a vertical seam to chains.

**14    Coyote Moon (5.9)**  Start at a block in the pit 15' left of the last route and 8' right of an oak tree. Zip past 4 bolts to chains.

**15    Spotted Eagle (5.10a)**  Rope up 25' left, at the left end of the pit and 10' right of a large, right-facing flake. Clip 4 bolts on your way to the chains.

## *The Trophy*

This sunny cliff redefines the word steep! To get there, walk 200 yards northwest from the parking lot on the main trail, past a white boulder in the main wash, to an old roadway. Follow the roadway for about another 200 yards to an obvious oak bush on the left side of the trail. Turn left off the roadway onto the trail that goes to Turtlehead. After about 200 yards, this footpath goes up over a dirt hump. Follow the trail along the top of the dirt mound until you reach white rocks. At this point, Turtlehead Trail turns right and goes down into the wash. Continue on the trail, which heads diagonally across the wash/valley toward white rocks and Turtlehead itself. The first white formation that the trail reaches is The Twinkie. Walk just past The Twinkie, then turn right off the trail toward a

Sandstone Quarry
Turtlehead ——▶
Avian Wall and The Trophy
Twinkie
To Calico Tank, Holiday Wall, etc.

The Trophy Area (as seen from near the Twinkie)

smooth, brown wave of rock (The Drive-In). Go northeast up the canyon about 150 yards to the obvious, overhanging wall on the left (north) side of the canyon. Routes are described from left to right. Total approach time is about 15 minutes.

**16    Shark Walk (5.13a)** Start just right of a cave and a scrub oak at the left (west) end of the main cliff. Climb past 6 bolts to the anchor. (Not shown.)

**17    Indian Giver (5.12c)** Begin 6' right of the last route and climb past 5 bolts to a chain anchor.

**18    Midnight Cowboy (5.13a)** Start 40' right of *Indian Giver* on a rounded pedestal. Trend out left along cracks, then up a brown streak past 9 bolts.

**19    Twilight of a Champion (5.13a)** An unsuccessful attempt to "steal" this route was made by a famous climber, hence the route name. Same start as the last route atop a pedestal. Climb pretty much straight up past 8 bolts to a chain anchor.

**20    Pet Shop Boy (5.12d)** Named after the first ascensionist's hairdo at the time. Begin 10' right of the last route and 8' left of a black recess at the base of the cliff. Stick-clip the first bolt, then climb straight back (!) past 5 more bolts.

**21    Keep Your Powder Dry (5.12b)** Rope up 6' right of the last route, at the left side of the central cave. Follow 9 bolts up very overhanging rock to chains.

**22    The Trophy (5.12c)** Makes *Fear and Loathing III* look like a slab climb! Starting 8' right, climb out the center of the cave along a right-slanting crack past 10 bolts to the anchor.

**23    Caught in the Crosshairs (5.12a)** Begin on a ledge 30' uphill of the central cave. Power past 7 bolts to the safety of the anchor.

**24    Dodging a Bullet (5.12a)** Start about 45' right of the central cave. Climb along vertical seams, clipping 5 bolts en route.

# Sandstone Quarry Northeast

## *Mass Production Wall*

From the Sandstone Quarry parking area, follow the trail markers for Calico Tank. The trail goes something like this: Walk 200 yards northwest from the parking area, past a white boulder in the main wash, to an old roadway. Follow the roadway for 250 yards past a bush and small drainage to an interpretive sign about Native Americans. Turn right (northeast) into the obvious pebbly wash and follow it between two rock formations. You reach some pine trees after another 140 yards.

The main wash curves left (north) at this point with a subsidiary wash continuing east. Follow this sandy wash east (there may be a trail marker here) for about 300 yards, then continue straight east along the same wash through a

The Trophy

canyon with red rock for another 300 yards. Just before the red layer of rock ends, you will see Mass Production Wall uphill to the left center (northeast). The cliff is in the shade most of the day and is primarily a white-colored rock with pine trees at its base. This approach takes about 15 minutes from the parking area. Routes are described from right to left, running uphill from the drainage bottom.

**25    Some Assembly Required (5.10c)**  Start behind a gnarled pine tree and climb along parallel, left-leaning seams, then up the face right of a cave. Follow 6 bolts to chain anchors.

**26    Kokopelli (5.10c PG)**  Named for the hunchbacked flute player commonly seen in Native American rock art. Begin 50' uphill of the last route and below the right center of a cave. Face-climb past bolts, then out the ceiling at a right-facing corner to chains.

**27    Parts Is Parts (5.8)**  Originally done with only traditional gear (5.8 X). Begin behind two pine trees 100' uphill of *Some Assembly Required.* Wander up the face past 4 bolts to reach the chain anchor.

**28    Battery Powered (5.9)**  Rope up 10' left of the last route and 10' right of a right-facing corner. Climb past 6 bolts to the chain anchor.

**29    Foreman Ferris (5.11b)**  This bolted route follows a thin seam that goes through the right side of the large varnished patch shaped roughly like Australia. There are 7 bolts on the climb.

**30**    **Trigger Happy (5.10a)** Start 90' uphill of *Battery Powered,* below a seam leading through the left edge of a large varnished patch shaped roughly like Australia. Scamper past 5 bolts to a chain anchor. A good route.

**31**    **Hit and Run (5.9)** Begin behind a pine tree with a broken top 10' left of *Trigger Happy*. Climb past 5 bolts to a chain anchor, keeping just right of a seam/crack.

## *Holiday Wall*

This crag has a number of very good sport routes that are in the sun most of the day. Total approach time is about 20 minutes. From the Sandstone Quarry parking area, follow the trail markers for Calico Tank. The trail goes something like this: Walk 200 yards northwest from the parking area, past a white boulder in the main wash, to an old roadway. Follow the roadway for 250 yards past a bush and small drainage to an interpretive sign about Native Americans. Turn right (northeast) into the obvious pebbly wash and follow it between two rock formations. You reach some pine trees after another 140 yards.

The main wash curves left (north) at this point with a subsidiary wash continuing east. Follow this sandy wash east (there may be a trail marker here) for about 300 yards, then continue straight east along the same wash through a

Mass Production Area

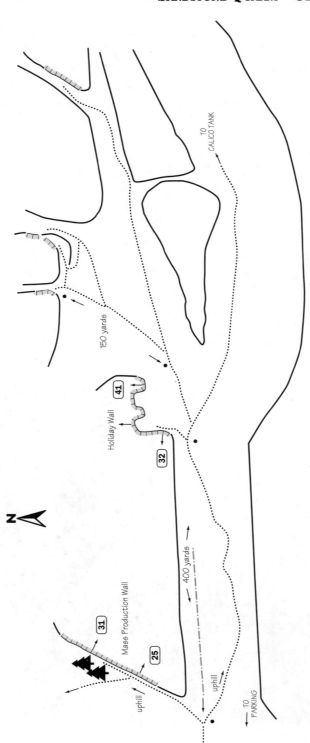

HOLIDAY WALL AREA

canyon with red rock for another 300 yards. Just before the red layer of rock ends, you will see Mass Production Wall uphill to the left center (northeast).

Continue up the main drainage beyond Mass Production Wall, heading slightly right to gain a trail that goes up along the hillside. About 200 yards beyond the end of the red rock, the trail drops down into a drainage and the red rock reappears. Continue up the valley another 200 yards to reach Holiday Wall, which is on the left (northeast) side of the drainage. The trail to Calico Tank continues for about another 500 yards. Routes at Holiday Wall are described from left to right as you approach up the drainage.

**32    Presents of Mind (5.12a)** Begin at the left edge of the wall, about 50' right of a medium-sized oak and below left-slanting cracks. Climb past 4 bolts with red hangers to an anchor.

**33    The Grinch (5.12c)** Start just right of the last route, at smooth, overhanging, varnished rock. Climb past 3 bolts (there were 4 bolts, but the first one is missing) to chains.

**34    Death before Decaf (5.12b)** Begin at a thin zigzag crack in varnished rock 15' right of *The Grinch*. Fire past 6 bolts to chains.

**35    Gift Rapped (5.11b)** "Given" as a Christmas present! Start 8' right of the last route, at a shallow, left-facing corner by a small pine and oak. Clip 6 bolts as you climb along seams to a chain anchor.

**36    Red Sky Mining (5.11a)** Climb past 7 bolts to chains, starting 3' right of *Gift Rapped*.

**37    Red Storm Rising (5.11b)** Rope up at the base of a chimney 3' right of the last route. Climb up along a left-facing flake/corner past 5 bolts to chains.

**38    When the Cat's Away (5.11b)** Rope up 15' right at the base of a buttress with a small ceiling at the bottom. Pull the ceiling and clip 6 bolts as you climb up small, opposing flake systems. A great route.

**39    Saddam's Mom (5.11d)** Could it be Mrs. Grinch? Begin 6' right of the last route, at the right arête of the buttress. Shoot past 6 bolts to a chain anchor.

**40    Moments to Memories (5.11a)** Start 40' right of *Saddam's Mom* and 30' right of a striking dihedral (a future testpiece) at the left arête of a short buttress. Climb the arête past 4 bolts to chains.

**41    Fast Moving Train (5.11a)** Begin just right of *Moments to Memories* and climb past 5 bolts up the right arête of the buttress.

# WILLOW SPRING

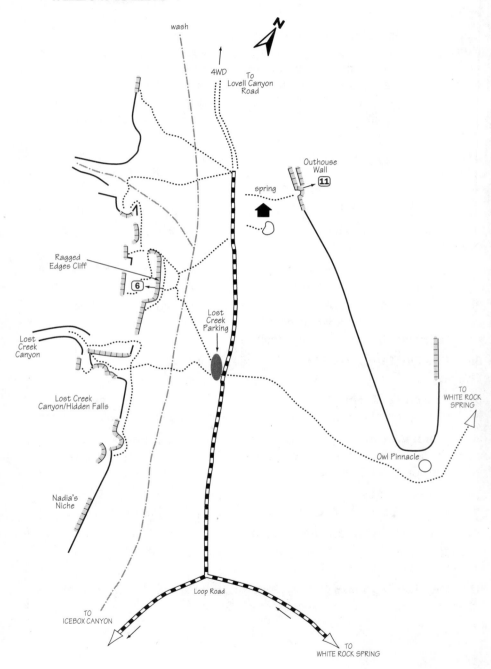

CHAPTER FIVE

# Willow Spring

While not as in vogue as The Gallery or Wall of Confusion, Willow Spring offers many short routes of good quality. The turnoff for Willow Spring is 7.3 miles along the scenic loop road. This spur road is paved for 0.6 mile; after that it's four-wheel-drive territory.

The routes described are one-pitch, though at times you may need two ropes to easily get back to your gear. Those longer convenience rappels are noted. The typical rack for Willow Spring includes a set of Friends, TCUs, and wired stoppers. It's mostly a traditional area.

At the end of the pavement is a picnic area on the right. There are a few picnic tables under the big cottonwood trees, a natural spring (no potable water, though), and an outhouse. Just to the right (east) of the outhouse building is some Native American rock art.

## Ragged Edges Cliff

This is probably the most obvious cliff in the Willow Spring area. Either park as for Lost Creek Canyon or continue driving down the spur road toward Willow Spring for another 0.3 mile (0.5 mile total from the scenic loop road). On the left side of the road is a large, varnished wall with an obvious vertical crack system in the center. This crack is the classic *Ragged Edges*. After deciding where to park, follow one of the clearly defined trails to the base of the cliff. The following routes are shaded most of the day.

**1    Kemosabe (5.10- PG)** An exciting climb. Bring small gear. Begin at the base of an arch 100' left of *Ragged Edges*. Climb the face and thin cracks up the arête of the arch to a bolt. Continue up the arête (scary), or weenie out and traverse off left, then up to the top. Walk off to the right (west) as on *Ragged Edges*.

**2    Tonto (5.5)** Climb the obvious crack in the slab that is 90' left of *Ragged Edges* and just right of the arch mentioned in *Kemosabe*. At the top, move out right onto the face or continue up the crack past a roof (5.7).

**3    Vision Quest (5.12d)** Start 75' left of *Ragged Edges* and just right of an

ugly chimney/corner. Climb up a short crack, then move slightly right to a bolt. Continue up the overhanging wall above, past 3 more bolts to a chain anchor. The second pitch climbs a left-leaning crack to the top (5.10+).

**4     Bodiddly (5.10 PG)** A very good route, but a tiny bit scary. Start 30' left of *Ragged Edges* on the left, front corner of the wall. Climb up the arête and face to a bolt, then follow more bolts up left (see variation) past a steep flake. Continue up the easy face above. Walk off right as for *Ragged Edges*. **Variation/**

**Bodacious (5.10)**: From the second bolt, it is possible to traverse straight left, then up past a bolt to rejoin the route. This was how this section of rock was first climbed. *Bodiddly* is the straighter (and perhaps more logical) line.

**5   Plan F (5.11- PG)** The initial finger crack is often done by itself, rapping off the anchor in the *Ragged Edges* crack. Begin below an obvious finger crack 8' left of *Ragged Edges*. Jam up the crack (5.10-), then angle left up the smooth, slippery face past a few bolts to the top.

**6   Ragged Edges (5.8)** The classic route at Willow Spring. Bring lots of large gear. Climb the central crack on the varnished wall in 2 short pitches. Walk off to the right (west), then back along the base of the crag.

**7   Chicken Eruptus (5.10 PG)** Named to commemorate a meal at Caesar's Palace the previous night! An excellent but sporty route for solid 5.10 leaders. Start 5' right of *Ragged Edges* and climb up a right-leaning ramp for 40' to horizontal cracks. Move out right to the nose, then climb straight up the face past a bolt to the summit. Bring #1.5 and #2 Friends for the belay.

**8   Gun Boy (5.11+ PG)** Start 30' right of *Ragged Edges* in a yellow band of rock. Climb past 1 bolt to a rounded, brown dihedral. Continue straight up the face, keeping just left of a black streak, passing 2 more bolts to the top. There's a rather scary section that requires some dicey moves off small RPs.

**9   Sheep Trail (5.10- PG)** Wonderful climbing, but make sure you're solid at the grade. This was originally rated 5.8! Begin 40' right of *Ragged Edges* at a black streak and a clearing in the vegetation. Weave up past numerous horizontal cracks to a shallow, left-facing corner about 50' up. Continue basically straight up the face, exiting the brown rock at a short, vertical crack. Belay on the terrace (small to medium Friends), then walk off right.

**10   Dense Pack (5.10 PG)** Another excellent but sporty route. Traverse out left on a ledge system 150' right of *Ragged Edges* to a right-facing corner. Lieback and stem up the corner, then swing out left (see variation). Weave up the varnished face above, angling slightly left. Belay on the terrace above, then walk off right. **Variation/Twelve Pack (5.10+)**: From atop the corner, follow an undercling flake out right. Climb up the face past 1 bolt to the terrace. (Not shown.)

## Outhouse Wall

To access this sunny cliff, park at the end of the pavement on the Willow Spring road. On the north (right) side of the road and above the outhouse building is a south-facing cliff. Go directly uphill for 50 yards to an alcove formed by a huge detached boulder. Many other routes have been done here, but only these few are listed. Routes are described from right to left. (No topo.)

**11    Tricks Are for Kids (5.10- PG13)** Bring your bag of tricks for this one. Start in the alcove above the outhouse building and climb a flake to a ledge at 20'. Continue up the left-leaning corner/crack above (cheater stones may be needed to get off the ledge), moving right when the crack doglegs. Walk off right (south).

**12    Spiderline (5.7 PG)** Start in the alcove as for *Tricks Are for Kids* and climb an easy, wide crack on the left to a platform 40' up. Climb the left edge of the varnish above, finishing at a notch in a small ceiling. Walk off right (south).

**13    Roasting Affair (5.10-)** The face just left of *Spiderline*, which has some fixed gear on it.

**14    Sin City (5.11- X)** This route climbs the left edge of the face, about 75' left of the *Spiderline* alcove. Start on a ledge and climb over a bulge, protecting in a right-leaning seam. Bring small wires.

**15    Jam Session (5.11-)** A shady overhanging crack around the corner and left of *Sin City*.

# CHAPTER SIX

# Icebox Canyon

The Icebox Canyon routes described here are primarily 1-pitch routes, although numerous multi-pitch routes exist. Drive 7.8 miles along the scenic loop road until you reach the Icebox Canyon parking area. A well-maintained trail leads from the parking lot into the canyon, and the routes are within 25 minutes of the road.

## *The Necromancer*

This dark, squat formation is on the left (south) side of the canyon and is clearly visible from the parking area. The formation is on the left side of a large

## ICEBOX CANYON

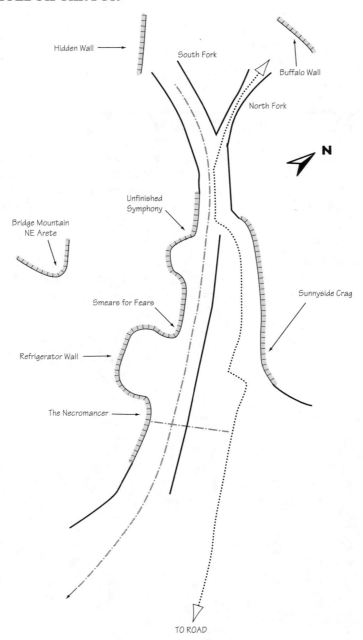

Hidden Wall

South Fork

Buffalo Wall

North Fork

N

Unfinished
Symphony

Bridge Mountain
NE Arete

Smears for Fears

Sunnyside Crag

Refrigerator Wall

The Necromancer

TO ROAD

# The Necromancer Area

amphitheater, and the routes lead to a huge terrace at the top of the formation. From the road, follow the main trail until you are even with the obvious orange roofs to the right (north) of the trail (just before you reach the right edge of Sunnyside Crag). Turn left (south) and go down a small drainage into the main wash (about 30 yards). Cross the main wash and follow a vague trail about 150 yards up the opposite hillside to a prominent, dark brown buttress. Again, this buttress forms the left side of an amphitheater that is clearly visible from the road. Routes are described from right to left (west to east), beginning at an obvious crack system near the right margin of the buttress. The routes are generally shady.

**1    Fold-Out (5.8)** This climbs the rightmost crack system on the buttress. Bring a normal rack and two ropes if you plan on rappelling. Excellent rock and good protection will get you to an anchor on a ledge about 140' up. If you do go to the top of the buttress, walk off left (toward the road).

**2    Sensuous Mortician (5.9)** This route is one of the best moderate routes at Red Rocks. Begin about 20' left of the *Fold-Out* crack at the next crack line. Climb the obvious crack to its top, then move right to a black streak. Wander up the black face to a ceiling, move left, then climb up to a 2-bolt belay. Bring lots of small gear and two ropes for the rappel.

**3    Black Magic Panties (5.10- R)** Great climbing, but rather scary. Carry gear up to 3", plus a bunch of long slings. This route starts about midway between *Sensuous Mortician* and *Hop Route*. Wander up the face to a fixed piton about 30' up. Continue weaving up the wall following the obvious weaknesses to a bolt about 100' up. Move up and left past another bolt to an obvious crack splitting the roof. Climb the crack through the roof and belay just above at horizontal cracks (#1.5 to #3 Friends for the anchor). Either traverse down and right to the anchor on *Sensuous Mortician* or go left and join *Hop Route*.

**4    Hop Route (5.7+)** The first pitch is very good, the rest a bit less interesting. Start about 10' left of *Black Magic Panties* at an obvious crack. **Pitch 1 (5.7)**: Climb a hand crack that is 15' right of a white, right-facing corner (see variation). Follow the crack as it veers left into the corner, then up that past a couple of chockstones to a belay ledge on the left. 100'. **Pitches 2 and 3:** Continue up the easy cracks to the top of the buttress. **Variation (5.7+)**: You can climb the corner directly. It's a bit harder than the hand crack. **Descent:** Walk off left (toward the road).

CHAPTER SEVEN

# Pine Creek Canyon

Many fine routes are located in this beautiful canyon. To reach the trailhead, drive 10.3 miles along the scenic loop road. The parking lot is signed and lies just off the road on your right. There are outhouses at the parking lot, and the trail is well maintained until the Pine Creek drainage splits.

From the parking lot, follow the obvious trail past the Fire Ecology Trail and an old homestead into the canyon proper (about a 15-minute walk). Ahead, the canyon is split into north and south drainages by a pyramid-shaped formation called Mescalito. The first routes described in this chapter are on the right (north) side of the canyon well before it is split by Mescalito. These routes are on Bridge Mountain, which separates Icebox Canyon from Pine Creek. Routes are

Pine/Juniper Canyons Overview

# PINE CREEK CANYON

**(MAP NOT TO SCALE)**

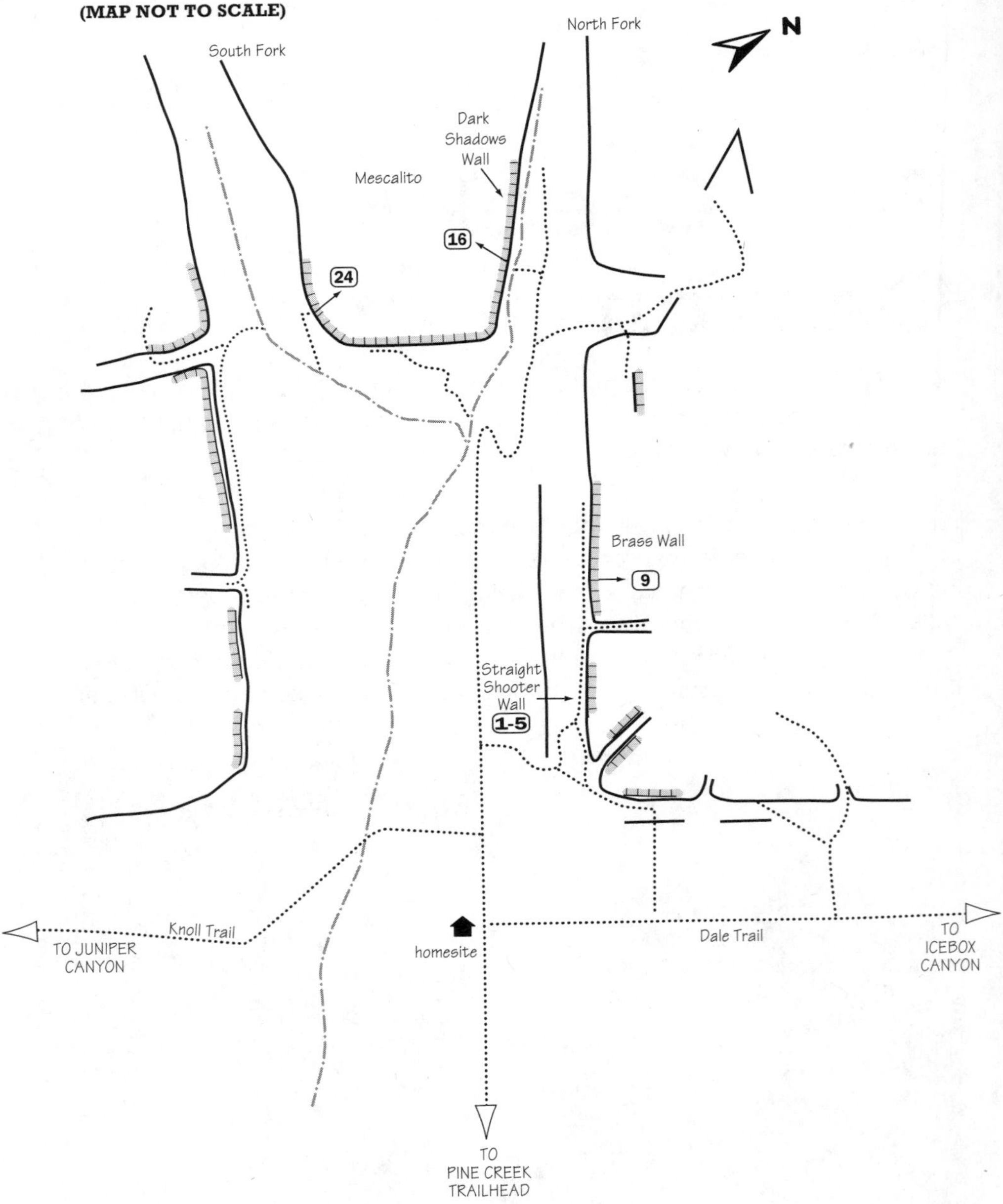

South Fork

North Fork

N

Dark
Shadows
Wall

Mescalito

16

24

Brass Wall

9

Straight
Shooter
Wall

1-5

TO JUNIPER
CANYON

Knoll Trail

homesite

Dale Trail

TO
ICEBOX
CANYON

TO
PINE CREEK
TRAILHEAD

described from right to left (counterclockwise) in the canyon, moving across Mescalito onto the south wall of Pine Creek.

## *Straight Shooter Wall*

As you enter the Pine Creek drainage, a short, red cliffband appears on the right. The Beer and Ice Gully is the obvious, huge cleft in the right wall of the canyon, and Straight Shooter Wall encompasses the climbs on the right side of this gully. To approach Straight Shooter Wall and Beer and Ice Gully, head off the trail by the homestead and skirt the right (east) end of the red cliffband. You can also hike directly up to Beer and Ice Gully, but this entails a bit of dicey soloing through the center of the red band. A well-beaten path runs along the base of the canyon wall in this area, which gets sun all day. The routes are described from right (east) to left (up canyon). The routes described here are located about 400' right of Beer and Ice Gully on a smooth, black face. Allow about 20 minutes for the approach.

**1      The Lazy Fireman (5.11a)** At the right end of a smooth, black face is a boulder/prow that protrudes from the cliff. On the left (west) face is a short, overhanging dihedral with 2 bolts. Continue up the face above (contrived) past 2 more bolts to a chain anchor. You may want to bring a #3 Friend or equivalent to place between the second and third bolts. (Not shown.)

**2      Sidewinder (5.11a)** Better than it first appears; it's quite technical. Start 20' left of the last route and just right of a striking finger crack up the smooth, black wall. Climb the slippery face past 6 bolts, following small flakes and seams to a shared rappel anchor.

**3      Straight Shooter (5.9+)** Climb the perfect, smooth, finger crack splitting the black face to a communal anchor 50' up. Bring wires, TCUs, and Friends up to #3.

**4      Slabba Dabba Do (5.11b PG13)** It's dicey getting to the first bolt, scary and cruxy above the third bolt. Begin about 10' left of *Straight Shooter* and smear up the glassy face past 3 bolts with homemade hangers to the ledge 50' up. You can set up a directional at the top of the pitch using the ¼" bolt and a #0 TCU.

**5      Forget Me Knot (5.11)** Shades of Lynn Hill, Ken Nichols, and other good climbers who have forgotten to tie into the climbing rope properly! Start at a thin, vertical seam 20' left of *Straight Shooter*. Climb the seam to a bolt, then up a left-facing flake directly above a ⅜" bolt to a ledge (5.10+; possible belay directional here using the ¼" bolt and a #0 TCU). Continue up the right-leaning crack (*Bird Crack*) on the upper wall to a rap anchor (5.11-).

Pine Creek Canyon
(North Side)

Beer and
Ice Gully

10  9  6
Brass Wall

5
Straight Shooter
Wall

3

To
The Mescalito

Scrambling

The Red Band

## Brass Wall

This is the section of cliff to the left (west) of Beer and Ice Gully, which is the obvious, huge cleft in the right wall of the canyon. As you enter the Pine Creek drainage, a short, red cliffband appears on the right. To approach Beer and Ice Gully, head off the trail by the homestead and skirt the right (east) end of the red cliffband. You can also hike directly up to Beer and Ice Gully itself, but this entails a bit of dicey soloing through the center of the red band. Allow about 25 minutes for the approach. Routes are described from right to left.

**6      Varnishing Point (5.8+)** Start 80' left of the bushy gully and 10' left of an oak tree, below an obvious crack that leads to the right side of a bushy ledge that is 70' up. Bring gear to a #4 Camalot and two ropes. **Pitch 1 (5.5)**: Climb the crack and huecos, stepping left to reach the bushy ledge. Belay in a cave. 70'. **Pitch 2 (5.8+)**: Climb the obvious, leftmost, left-facing corner past a ceiling (crux) to the top of the huge varnished flake. 70'. **Descent:** Rappel with two ropes.

**7      Fungus Folks (5.11+)** Start 50' left of *Varnishing Point* under the center of the bushy ledge that is 70' up. Climb the thin, vertical seam up the varnished face to the bushy ledge.

PINE CREEK CANYON

BRASS WALL

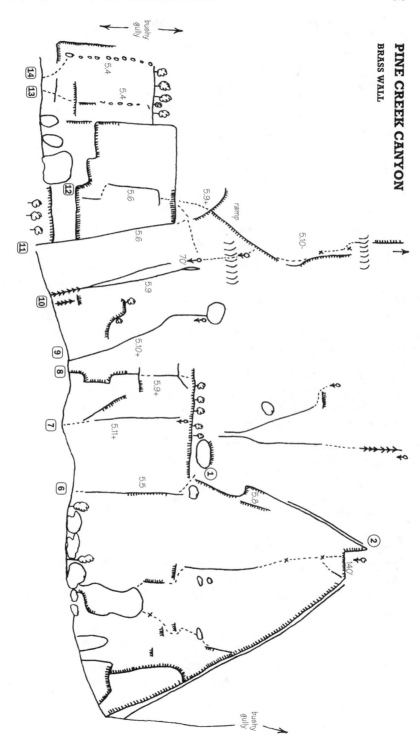

bushy
gully

5.4

14
13

5.4

5.6

12

5.9+

ramp

5.6

5.10-

11

70'

5.9

10

5.10+

9

8

5.9+

7

5.11+

5.5

6

1

5.8

2

140'

bushy
gully

**8    Bush Pilots (5.9+)**   Begin   at a right-facing corner 20' left of the last climb. Climb the corner to a prominent ceiling, then follow the crack above to the left end of the bushy ledge.

**9    Mushroom People (5.10+)**   Start about 15' left of the last route, directly below the left edge of a bushy ledge about 70' up. Climb an obvious, left-angling seam up slippery, black rock to a rap anchor just below a huge hueco. Two ropes are needed for the rappel.

**10    Topless Twins (5.9)**   Rope up below a series of short dihedrals leading to thin, parallel, black cracks 50' left of *Mushroom People*. Climb a dihedral and the right-hand crack to a rappel station 70' up, then zip back to the ground with one rope. You'll need a good selection of wires and TCUs for this fun route.

**11    Heavy Spider Karma (5.6)**   Worthwhile. Start 10' to the left of the last route, at the base of a prominent hand crack leading to a ledge. Traverse right from the ledge to the *Topless Twins* anchor and rappel.

**12    Snivler (5.5 R)**   A good route. Rope up 20' left of *Heavy Spider Karma* at a boulder below a ceiling. Step right off the boulder then go straight up a crack to a ledge. Step left and climb a series of pockets up the varnished face to a ledge. Step right and climb a short face to the big ledge. Traverse right to the *Topless Twins* anchor or continue up *Raptor* (not described here).

**13    Zen and the Art of Web Spinning (5.4)**   Start 30' left of the last route on the left side of large boulders below a low-angle, Swiss-cheese face and 8' left of an obvious, left-facing corner. Climb the left-facing corner and Swiss-cheese rock to a tree-covered ledge.

**14    Arachnoworld (5.4)**   Climb the easy, huecoed face 20' left of *Zen and the Art of Web Spinning* (and near the arête) to the tree ledge.

# North Fork of Pine Creek Canyon

## Dark Shadows Wall

The next routes are located on the north face of Mescalito, the pyramid-shaped formation splitting the canyon into two drainages. The rock is of excellent quality, rivaling the best in Black Velvet Canyon. Bring two ropes to get off all of these shady routes.

From the Pine Creek parking lot, follow the trail into Pine Creek Canyon, going past the Fire Ecology Trail and an old homesite. When the canyon forks, take the right (north) fork. The trail becomes a bit braided at this point. The best route is to head uphill on the right (north) side of the canyon for about 100 feet (above the red band of rock), then head left (west), contouring along the hillside on a relatively level trail. Follow the trail up canyon for about 600 yards, keeping well

# PINE CREEK CANYON
## DARK SHADOWS AREA

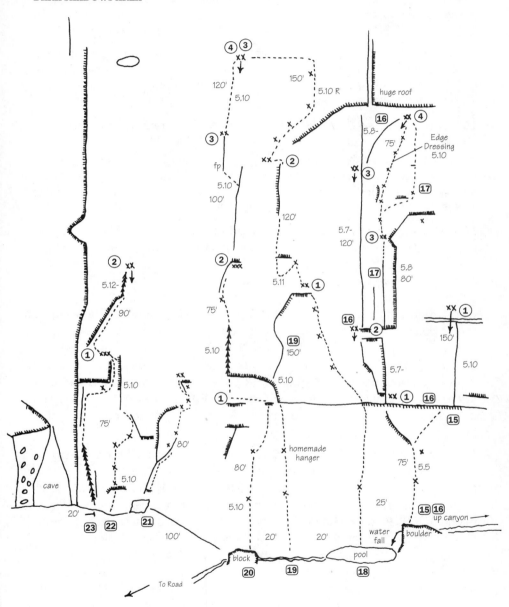

above the drainage bottom. Continue up-canyon until you are even with the farthest large pine trees in the drainage. You should now be able to clearly see the varnished north face of Mescalito. Pine Creek runs along the base of the wall here, and the surrounding vegetation is surprisingly lush and varied.

The climbs described next are all located on this varnished section of cliff and are described from right to left (down canyon). You may need to head down to the drainage bottom from the trail to see the pools noted in the route descriptions. Total approach time is about 30 minutes.

**15    Slot Machine (5.10 PG)** Those with small fingers will be rewarded on this worthwhile pitch. Start as for *Dark Shadows* atop a flat boulder at the right edge of the pool at the base of the cliff. Bring small RPs and gear up to a #3 Friend. Climb easily past 2 bolts to the base of a left-leaning ramp (as for *Dark Shadows*). Continue straight up a thin seam in a steep, varnished wall, passing 1 bolt to the anchor. Rappel with two ropes. 150'.

**16    Dark Shadows (5.8-)** One of the best 5.8 routes at Red Rocks and a popular soap opera in its time. The climb goes to the top of Mescalito, but only the first four pitches are described here. Bring a variety of gear and be prepared to have fun. Start on a flat boulder atop a small waterfall at the right edge of a pool and below a huge, black dihedral system capped by a giant roof. Good belay ledges on each pitch. **Pitch 1 (5.5 PG13)**: Face-climb up and right past 2 bolts to a left-leaning ramp that leads to the base of a varnished corner. Two-bolt belay anchor. 75'. **Pitch 2 (5.7-)**: Climb the clean, varnished, right-facing corner above, moving left to a belay ledge and an anchor. (Pitches 1 and 2 may be combined.) 75'. **Pitch 3 (5.7-)**: Stem up the beautiful dihedral to a ledge with two different belay anchors. 120'. **Pitch 4 (5.8-)**: Climb the right-curving crack in the right wall to another anchor belay under the giant roof. 75'. **Descent:** Three rappels using two ropes to get down.

**17    Chasing Shadows (5.8+ PG13)** Good climbing on this one. Bring gear to a #4 Camalot for the second pitch of the route. The second pitch was originally done with only the silver bolt! **Pitch 1 (5.7-)**: Climb *Dark Shadows* to the belay at the base of the huge corner (this can be done in one or two pitches). 150'. **Pitch 2 (5.8+)**: From the *Dark Shadows* belay, move back right to the right-hand (and widest) of two vertical crack systems. Follow this past a wide section to a 2-bolt belay. 80'. **Pitch 3 (5.8+ PG13)**: Continue straight up the vague arête past a couple of bolts with black hangers, then move out right above a ceiling to a bolt with a silver hanger (variation exists). Wander up and slightly right along the arête (wires, TCUs, small Friends) to the belay on *Dark Shadows* below the huge *Heart of Darkness* roof. 120'. **Variation/Edge Dressing (5.10 PG)**: Move up left to a bolt, then up past 6 more bolts to the belay on *Dark Shadows* below the right edge of the huge *Heart of Darkness* roof.

Bring a #3 Friend to supplement the bolts. **Descent:** Do three rappels using two ropes, as per *Dark Shadows*.

**18    Sandstone Sandwich (5.10c PG13)**  Don't bite off more than you can chew! A wonderful bolted face-climb between the first pitches of *Dark Shadows* and *Excellent Adventure*. Rappel with two ropes from the first belay on *Excellent Adventure*, or continue up that route. Bring #1 and #1.5 Friends.

**19    Excellent Adventure (5.11 R)**  Perhaps the best route on the wall. Really scary on the last pitch for both the leader and follower. Start 20' right of *Risky Business* and 25' left of *Dark Shadows* at the left edge of the deeper pool at the base of the cliff. **Pitch 1 (5.10)**: Climb to the right end of the arching ceiling on *Risky Business*, passing 2 bolts with homemade hangers en route. Follow the arching ceiling left for 15', then pull the ceiling. Intimidating climbing leads left to a crack system. Follow this up and slightly right past an overhang to a belay stance with bolts. 150'. **Pitch 2 (5.11)**: Go up from the belay, then make tricky moves down and left (bolts). Climb up the right side of a vague arête, stepping back out left to a belay anchor. 120'. **Pitch 3 (5.10 R)**: Get ready! Follow bolts up and right along the lip of the giant roof, then straight up. Eventually, you can angle back left to the final rap station on *Risky Business* and rappel the route. Whew!

**20    Risky Business (5.10+ PG)**  Certainly as good as the movie, maybe better! Begin 20' left of the last route and 100' right of *Parental Guidance* where the stream runs along the base of the cliff and directly in front of some large blocks. **Pitch 1 (5.10)**: Up a short, left-facing flake, then face-climb past 2 bolts. Move slightly right to a flake (scary) then easily up left to a belay at the left end of an arching ceiling. 80'. **Pitch 2 (5.10)**: Follow the shallow dihedral above the left edge of the ceiling, then continue along a seam to a belay station under a small ceiling. 75'. **Pitch 3 (5.10)**: Step left and climb to a bolt. Head back right to a crack, which is climbed until you can go left to a corner with a fixed piton. The bolted belay is above. 100'. **Pitch 4 (5.10+)**: Continue up the varnished wall above past numerous bolts to another rap station. 120'. **Descent:** Rappel with two ropes.

**21    Short Circuit (5.11 PG)**  A very sustained and sporty pitch. Unless you have a lot of talent and a cool head, you may short out! Bring a couple of tiny TCUs, a large stopper, and a couple of long slings. Start atop a boulder 20' right of *Parental Guidance* and climb a shallow, right-leaning flake/corner past a fixed peg and 2 bolts to a ledge. Step right, then make very hard moves past another bolt to a short corner and the belay anchor. Rappel with one rope.

**22    Parental Guidance (5.12- PG13)**  The first pitch is worth doing by itself. Bring numerous small Friends, TCUs, and wires for the first pitch. Start about 100' left of *Risky Business* and 8' right of *Lethal Weapon* at a small block leaning against the cliff. **Pitch 1 (5.10)**: Climb the face to an overlap 15' up (bolt), then continue past 2 more bolts to a stance (bolt). Angle up left to an obvious, vertical flake. At the top of the flake, step left to a communal belay. 75'. **Pitch 2 (5.12-)**: Face-climb past bolts to a right-leaning flake/crack, and pull past this into a shallow dihedral. 90'. **Descent:** Rap the route.

**23    Lethal Weapon (5.12)**  The left (east) margin of this wall is defined by a huge, right-facing chimney/corner system, the bottom of which forms a cave (this chimney/corner system is *Negro Blanco*). Start 20' right of the cave in a cleared area that is below several small corners and a huge flake/chimney system. Climb the easy, bigger dihedral to the base of a gaping chimney, then angle right up a corner to a roof. Traverse right under the roof (bolt) and follow a flake to a belay station.

# South Fork of Pine Creek Canyon

## *Mescalito, South Face*

From the Pine Creek parking lot, follow the trail into Pine Creek Canyon, going past the Fire Ecology Trail and an old homesite. When the canyon forks, take the left (south) drainage for about 75 yards, then follow a trail on the right (Mescalito) side of the creekbed. Continue on this vague trail around the toe of the south buttress, keeping well above the drainage bottom and passing numerous crack systems. A well-worn trail up a talus slope brings you to the base of this sunny route. Total approach time is about 30 minutes.

**24    Cat in the Hat (5.6+)**  A wonderful, moderate route that can be done during colder weather. Carry a good selection of gear, including long slings and two ropes for rappelling. This route is located on the south side of the Mescalito, the pyramid-shaped formation splitting Pine Creek Canyon. Start at a crack system that is 75' left of a prominent chimney. Directly uphill from the start of the climb is a bushy gully that leads to steep, broken, brown rock. **Pitch 1 (5.5)**: Climb an obvious, slightly left-slanting crack past numerous huecos, moving right to a ledge with a small bush and slings around a horn. 90'. Climb the left-slanting fist crack above to another ledge, then continue up the corner/chimney directly above to belay on a sloping terrace. 150'. **Pitch 2 (5.5)**: From the right-center portion of the terrace, climb a steep, black wall to a ledge. Step left and follow a left-facing corner to a ledge with a tree (many rappel slings on the tree). 60'. **Pitch 3 (5.6)**: A great pitch. From the first ledge above the rappel tree, climb the black face just left of a left-facing corner along a thin crack. Move left just below a white ceiling and follow a finger crack up the wall to a ledge. Belay on the highest ledge at slings around a block. 110'. **Pitch 4 (5.3)**: Step down and traverse around right to a series of blocky ledges with slings. This pitch can be combined with Pitch 5. 50'. **Pitch 5 (5.6+)**: Climb the beautiful crack up the center of the black

**PINE CREEK CANYON**

CAT IN THE HAT (5.6+)

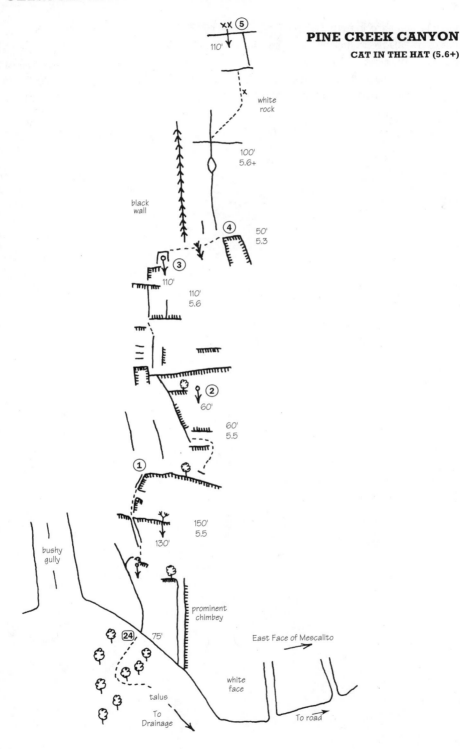

xx ⑤
110'

white
rock

100'
5.6+

black
wall

④ 50'
5.3

③
110'

110'
5.6

② 60'

60'
5.5

①

150'
5.5

130'

bushy
gully

prominent
chimbey

24 75'

East Face of Mescalito

white
face

talus

To
Drainage

To road

wall. When it ends in the white rock, angle right around a corner to a bolt, then up the crack above to the top (2-bolt belay). 100'. **Descent:** Rappel with two ropes as follows. First do a 110-foot rappel to the block atop pitch 3. Follow this with another 110-foot rappel to tree. Then do a 60-foot rappel to a terrace. Next scramble down the terrace to bolts on a ledge. Last, a 130-foot rappel from bolts gets you to the ground.

CHAPTER EIGHT

# Juniper Canyon

It is probably best to approach Juniper Canyon by parking at the Pine Creek parking area, located 10.3 miles along the scenic loop road. A spur road leads off the loop road to access Oak Creek Canyon and this may also be used to access Juniper Canyon. From the Pine Creek parking area, follow the well-marked Pine Creek Canyon Trail past the old homesite, then take the Knoll Trail that runs south in front of the escarpment. Various social trails also lead directly across the desert from the Fire Ecology Trail to Juniper Canyon. Once you enter Juniper Canyon, follow the main drainage to avoid dense scrub oak. The selected climbs are scattered throughout the canyon—each route has its own

Juniper Canyon
Overview

Rainbow Mountain

Rainbow Wall

Brownstone Wall

1st Creek Canyon

Mescalito

Juniper Canyon

Pine Creek Canyon

# JUNIPER CANYON

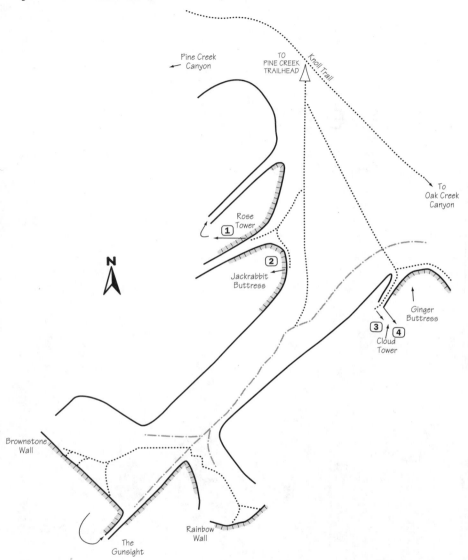

detailed description to find its start. Routes are described from right to left (north to south).

## Rose Tower

Rose Tower is a separate formation from the right (north) wall of Juniper Canyon. The top of the formation is light pink in color, hence the name.

From the Pine Creek parking area, follow the Pine Creek Canyon Trail down the hill and past the Fire Ecology Trail and old homestead. Turn left off the Pine Creek Trail onto the marked hiking trail that runs south along the base of the escarpment (the Knoll Trail). This trail crosses the Pine Creek drainage, then angles up a red hillside to flat ground. Follow this trail south to a point just before the mouth of Juniper Canyon. Head up right along a climber's trail into a tree-filled gully to the left (west) of Rose Tower. This approach takes about 45 minutes.

**1**   **Olive Oil (5.7 PG)** A slick route. Bring large gear to protect the last two pitches. Scramble about 200 yards up the tree-filled gully to the base of the route, which is in the sun all day. Start the climb at the base of a left-leaning chimney/corner with an obvious tree about 150' up. The base of the chimney/corner forms somewhat of a cave. **Pitch 1 (5.7 PG)**: Climb up the left-leaning ramp just left of the ugly chimney/corner to a tree and ledge (rap anchors here). 150'. **Pitch 2 (5.7)**: Slither up a short chimney, then up the obvious finger-and-hand crack about 15' right of a large, right-facing corner. Belay in the crack when you run out of rope. 150'. **Pitch 3 (5.6)**: Continue up the crack and face, eventually moving left into the right-facing corner. Belay on a large ledge just left of the corner. 120'. **Pitch 4 (5.5)**: Traverse right about 20' and follow the central crack. At the end of the pitch, move right into the left-facing corner and belay. 150'. **Pitch 5 (5.4)**: Continue up the corner for 30' to a huge ledge on the right. Walk about 25' to the right. 55'. **Pitch 6 (5.7 PG)**: Angle up right across the face into the huge dihedral above. Continue up this until you've run out of rope. 150'. **Pitch 7 (5.6)**: Continue up the corner to the top. 150'. **Descent:** Scramble about 150' up slabs, then walk to the top of Rose Tower. Walk left (west) to a notch, then drop down right (north) into the gully. A typically bushy but easy descent to the valley floor (toward the road) follows.

## Jackrabbit Buttress

Jackrabbit Buttress is located just left of Rose Tower toward the main portion of Juniper Canyon. When viewed from the Pine Creek parking area, Jackrabbit Buttress forms what appears to be the right skyline of Juniper Canyon.

From the Pine Creek parking area, follow the Pine Creek Canyon Trail down the hill and past the Fire Ecology Trail and old homestead. Turn left off the Pine

# JUNIPER CANYON
## ROSE TOWER
## OLIVE OIL (5.7 PG)

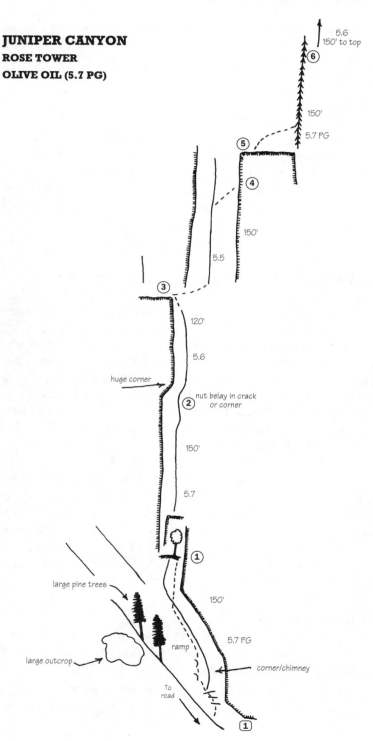

5.6
150' to top

150'

5.7 PG

5.5

150'

120'

5.6

huge corner

nut belay in crack
or corner

150'

5.7

large pine trees

150'

ramp

5.7 PG

large outcrop

corner/chimney

To
road

Creek Trail onto the marked Knoll Trail, which runs south along the base of the escarpment. This trail crosses the Pine Creek drainage, then angles up a red hillside to flat ground. Follow this trail south to a point just before the mouth of Juniper Canyon. Head up right along a climber's trail, aiming for a tree-filled gully to the left (west) of Rose Tower (a separate formation from the right/north wall of Juniper Canyon). At the mouth of the gully, head left (south) along the base of the cliff for about 200 yards. This approach takes about 45 minutes.

Olive Oil

**2      Geronimo (5.7)**  This route has become very popular—it is of good quality. Bring wires, TCUs, and cams up to #4. Carry two ropes and some extra sling or rope material for the descent. The route starts in a brush-filled gully below an obvious dogleg crack and is in the sun all day. **Pitch 1 (5.7)**: Climb the dogleg crack to a large ledge with boulders. 155'. **Pitch 2 (5.6)**: Move to the left side of the ledge and climb a thin crack, which leads to a ledge (optional belay here). Climb the face above the big ledge to one of a couple of belay stances. 150'. **Pitch 3 (5.3)**: Continue up onto a big terrace, then move left to the base of a black face. Belay from bushes on the terrace. 50'. **Pitch 4 (5.7)**: Climb the black face, aiming for a dihedral near the skyline. Belay on the skyline at a small stance (cams). 150'. **Pitch 5 (5.6)**: Step up and right from the belay onto a sloping shelf (exposed). Climb the lower-angle face to the summit. 90'. **Descent:** Rappel as follows: From a bolt anchor on the summit, rappel straight down a dark wall to the highest point of the bushy terrace atop pitch 3 (165'). Scramble down on the terrace to the top of a gully. This gully should be just right (north) of where you came up onto the bushy terrace. About 10' down the gully is a large chockstone with slings around it. Rappel with one rope down the gully/chimney to another chockstone. Be careful not to lose your rope in the crack! Rappel with one rope from the second chockstone down to a ledge with a tree. Rappel from the tree to the ground, making sure that your ropes will pull.

## *Cloud Tower*

The next routes are located on Cloud Tower, which sits near the mouth of Juniper Canyon. Cloud Tower has a distinctive red summit and is located at the top of a prominent, right-leaning ramp. The ramp and the tower are clearly visible from the Pine Creek parking area on the left (south) side of Juniper Canyon. These routes generally face north and consequently receive very little sun. It takes about an hour to reach the top of the ramp from either the Pine Creek or Oak Creek parking areas. If you approach from Oak Creek, contour along the base of the mountain to reach the base of the ramp rather than trying to angle up across the hillside to intersect the ramp.

**3      Cloud Tower (5.11+)**  Called *The Astroman* of Red Rocks by some; the final pitch is one of the very best in the area. Bring a good selection of wires, extra TCUs, a full set of cams, and two ropes. Start about 200' down from the top of the ramp and 100' right of *Crimson Chrysalis*. **Pitch 1 (5.8)**: Climb a left-facing corner to a belay. 150'. **Pitch 2 (5.8)**: Continue up the corner and belay on a bushy ledge. 100'. **Pitch 3 (5.10-)**: Power up the beautiful straight-in hand crack. 150'. **Pitch 4 (5.11+)**: Stem up the right-facing, right-leaning corner with a tips crack in its back to a ledge with 2 bolts and a loose block. Bring lots of TCUs for this crux pitch. 120'. **Pitch 5 (5.10)**: Pull over a roof, then up a hand-and-fist crack in the middle of a face to a belay ledge. 140'. **Pitch 6 (5.10+)**:

# JUNIPER CANYON
**JACKRABBIT BUTTRESS**
**GERONIMO (5.7)**

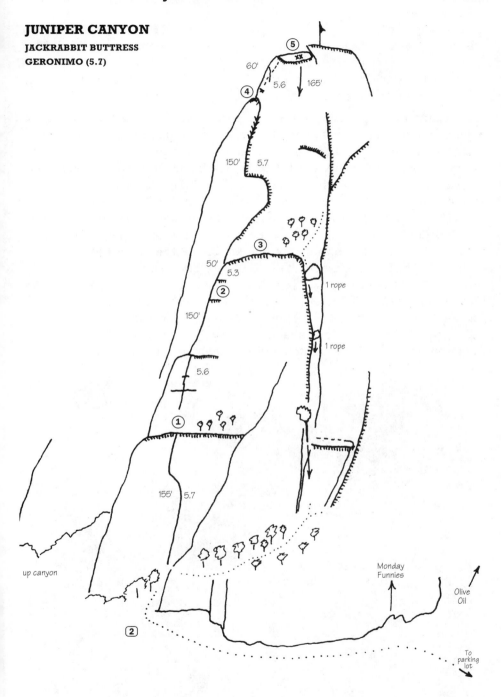

60'

5.6    165'

150'    5.7

50'

5.3

150'

1 rope

1 rope

5.6

155'    5.7

up canyon

Monday
Funnies

Olive
Oil

To
parking
lot

Struggle up a scary off-width to the top of the tower. 60'. **Pitch 7 (5.11+)**: Climb the incredible right-facing corner with a hand-and-finger crack in its back. The crux is at the top of the pitch, reaching the bolts. 160'. **Descent:** Rappel straight down (not down the route), keeping right of the tower. It'll be a bit dicey to reach a couple of the anchors even with 60-meter ropes.

**4      Crimson Chrysalis (5.8+)** A superb route that requires some crack climbing skills and stamina. Bring two ropes and a good selection of bigger gear. Start about 100' downhill (west and up canyon) from the top of the prominent approach ramp. **Pitch 1 (5.7)**: Climb the obvious crack and right-facing corner to a belay anchor. 125'. **Pitch 2 (5.8-)**: Continue up the crack/corner past 4 bolts to another anchor in a recess. 90'. **Pitch 3 (5.8+)**: Jam up the same fissure past 3 bolts and a steep section to a hanging belay from bolts. 60'. **Pitch 4 (5.8)**: Worm up a chimney (bolt), then follow lower-angle thin cracks through two bulges to a belay ledge. 90'. **Pitch 5 (5.8+)**: Climb a finger-and-hand crack past 1 bolt to a belay station at a small, good ledge. 90'. **Pitch 6 (5.6)**: Go up left past 2 bolts, then up and right past 3 more bolts to the anchor. 90'. **Pitch 7 (5.6+)**: Nine bolts will get you to the belay, which is 25' into the red rock. 110'. **Pitch 8 (5.7)**: Climb up 25' to a ramp (bolt), traverse straight right, then climb up left along a ramp. Climb the chocolate-colored face past 3 more bolts to the belay. 75'. **Pitch 9 (5.8)**: Climb up and right on a plated wall

Rainbow Mountain

Cloud Tower

Cloud Tower Area

Original Route
Rainbow Wall

4

approach

To
Brownstone and
Rainbow Walls

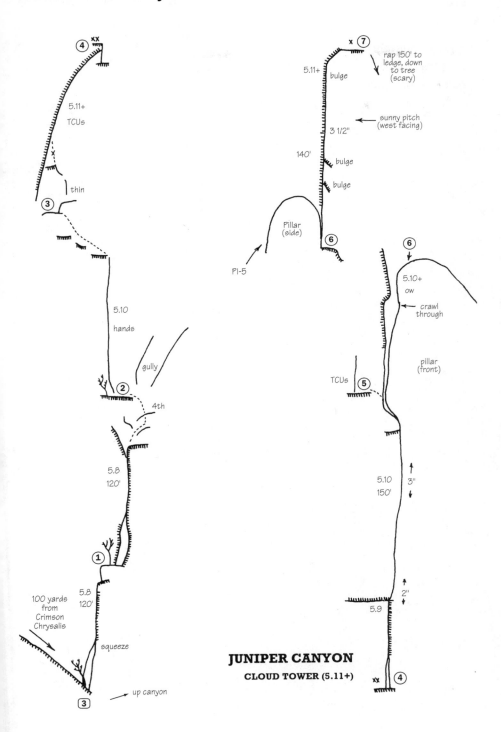

4

xx

5.11+
TCUs

x

thin

3

5.10

hands

gully

2

4th

5.8
120'

1

100 yards
from
Crimson
Chrysalis

5.8
120'

squeeze

up canyon

3

x  7

5.11+        bulge

rap 150' to
ledge, down
to tree
(scary)

3 1/2"

sunny pitch
(west facing)

140'        bulge

bulge

Pillar
(side)

6

Pl-5

6

5.10+
ow

crawl
through

TCUs   5

pillar
(front)

5.10        3"
150'

5.9

2"

xx   4

**JUNIPER CANYON**
**CLOUD TOWER (5.11+)**

**JUNIPER CANYON**

**CRIMSON CHRYSALIS (5.8+)**

**(NOT ALL BOLTS SHOWN)**

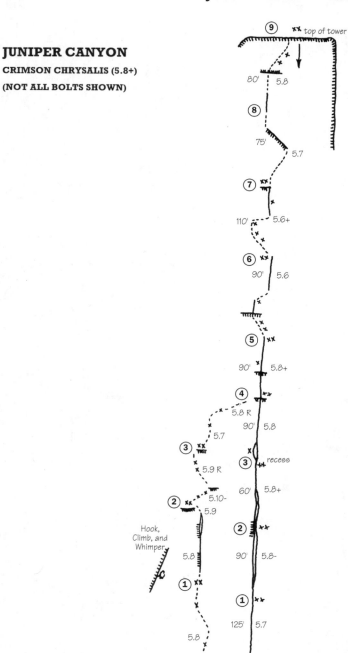

past 4 bolts and a ceiling to the shoulder of the tower. 80'. **Descent:** Rappel with two ropes, being careful not to get the ropes stuck in the crack.

**5      Hook, Climb, and Whimper (5.10- R)** This route climbs the face to the left of the first 4 pitches of *Crimson Chrysalis*. Bring wires, TCUs, extra cams up to #2.5, and two ropes. **Pitch 1 (5.8)**: Climb the face and discontinuous cracks past 2 bolts to an anchor. **Pitch 2 (5.9)**: Climb a crack and corner system above the belay to its top (5.8). Move up and left to a belay. **Pitch 3 (5.10-)**: Go up and right past 3 bolts to a ledge (crux). Angle up and left from the ledge **(5.9 R)** past a bolt to the belay anchor. **Pitch 4 (5.8 R)**: Wander up the face above the belay to a bolt, then traverse straight right past another bolt to the fourth belay on *Crimson Chrysalis*. **Descent:** Rappel *Crimson Chrysalis* with two ropes.

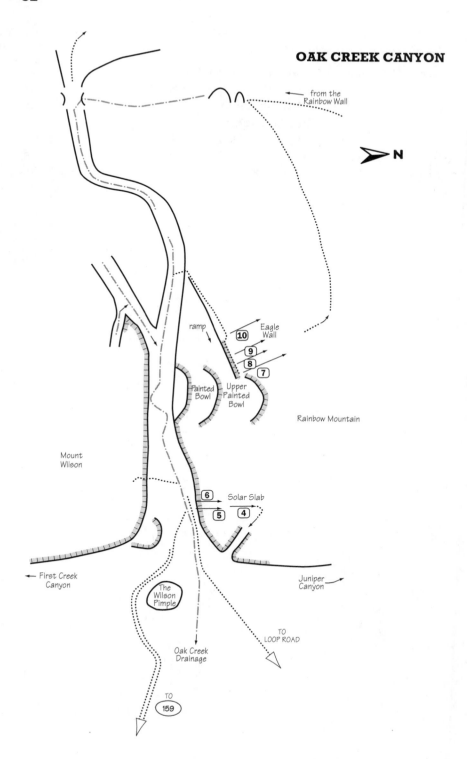

**OAK CREEK CANYON**

from the
Rainbow Wall

N

ramp

10  Eagle
Wall

9

8

7

Painted
Bowl

Upper
Painted
Bowl

Rainbow Mountain

Mount
Wilson

6  Solar Slab

5      4

First Creek
Canyon

Juniper
Canyon

The
Wilson
Pimple

TO
LOOP ROAD

Oak Creek
Drainage

TO
159

CHAPTER NINE

# Oak Creek Canyon

This canyon is on a par with Black Velvet, harboring some of the best routes at Red Rocks; however, the approaches are generally much longer than Black Velvet. Routes are all on the right (north) wall of the canyon and are described from right (east) to left (up canyon) starting at the Solar Slab Area.

There are two ways to approach the climbs in Oak Creek Canyon. 1) Start at the Oak Creek Canyon parking area, which is located at the end of a spur road

**Mount Wilson
& Oak Creek Canyon**

Mount Wilson

First Creek
Canyon

Rainbow
Mountain

Rainbow Buttress

Wilson Pimple

4

To Loop Road

To 159

leading off the scenic loop road. While this trailhead and adjoining trail provide a faster approach than the old Oak Creek Road, the opening and closing times of the loop road may prove problematic for those attempting the longer routes. From the parking area it is about a 30-minute hike to the mouth of the canyon. 2) It is also possible to walk the old Oak Creek Road, which begins at the old Oak Creek Campground. The old campground is located 1.4 miles south (toward Blue Diamond) on Nevada 159 from the exit of the scenic loop road. From the old campground, walk 1.5 miles along the obvious roadbed to the mouth of the canyon.

Both approaches go by the huge dirt mound situated at the canyon mouth. The mound is called Wilson Pimple. These trails then drop into the main Oak Creek drainage, which is followed some distance up-canyon.

## Solar Slab Area

On the far right (north) side of the canyon is a huge, obvious gully running about 500 feet up the cliff to the base of a white face. The gully is *Solar Slab Gully* and the white face above is *Solar Slab*. About 200 feet to the right (toward the road) of the gully is a large pinnacle with a huge boulder on the summit. This is *The Friar*. To the left of *Solar Slab Gully* is a huge, varnished right-facing corner. This is the line of *Beulah's Book*. These routes are in the sun and take about 45 minutes to approach from the Oak Creek Canyon parking area on the loop road.

From the Wilson Pimple, follow the old roadbed and/or a trail up toward the canyon until the trail drops into the streambed. Walk up the streambed about 150 yards, then follow a trail 200 yards up to the base of the routes. The trail ascends the hillside about 75 yards left (west) of the red rock band in the hillside.

**1     Red Zinger (5.10+)** This route is a classic. Bring a bunch of medium-sized cams and some muscle. About 200' right (east) of *The Friar* pinnacle is an alcove that faces up-canyon (west). This alcove is on the right (north) side of the canyon a few hundred yards from the mouth. *Red Zinger* climbs a striking crack in a small, left-facing corner in this area. The route is not visible from below, but once you're near the base of *Solar Slab Gully*, you can't miss it. **Pitch 1 (5.10+)**: Climb the crack and corner to a ledge with an anchor. **Pitch 2 (5.10+)**: Continue up the crack, then traverse left under a ceiling to a right-facing corner. Follow this corner up to an anchor. **Descent:** Rappel.

**Note:** The corner just left of *Red Zinger* is supposed to be 5.9.

**2     The Friar (5.9+ PG)** The first pitch of this route is excellent and a good way to round out a day. This route climbs the front (south) face of a 250' pillar

that is to the right of *Solar Slab Gully*. A trail leads over from the gully to the base of the route. Rope up below a varnished dihedral that begins about 10' off the ground. **Pitch 1 (5.7)**: Climb up onto a ledge at the base of a corner, then climb the varnished dihedral to an obvious ledge. 100'. **Pitch 2 (5.7)**: From the lower of two ledges (see Variations 1 and 2), move right and climb an obvious crack system to another ledge with an anchor. 90'. **Pitch 3 (5.6 R)**: From the highest

86

**OAK CREEK**
THE FRIAR (5.9+ PG)

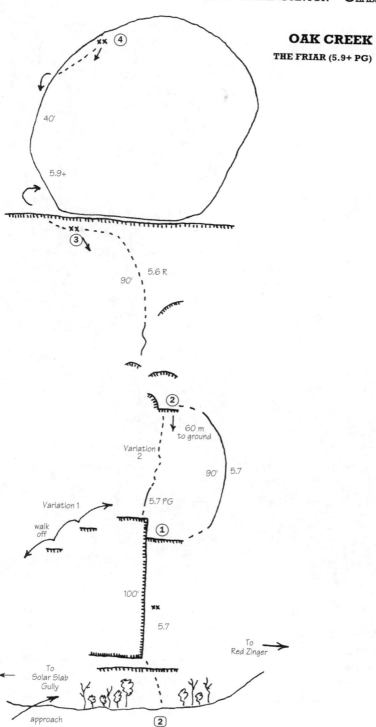

ledge, climb up the face along vertical seams to the base of the summit boulder. Go left (west) past an anchor to a large ledge between the boulder and the main canyon wall. 90'. **Pitch 4 (5.9+ PG)**: Starting on the overhanging west arête of the boulder, climb up and right (scary), then up to the top. 40'. **Variation 1:** From the higher of the two ledges, you can walk off left (toward *Solar Slab Gully*). This can also be used to toprope the first pitch. **Variation 2 (5.7 PG)**: From the higher ledge, climb straight up the scary face, keeping about 20' left of the normal Pitch 2 crack. **Descent:** Rappel with one rope as follows: Rappel from an anchor atop the summit boulder. Then rappel from the anchor just under the summit boulder to the anchor atop Pitch 2. And finally, with a 60-meter rope, you can just barely make it from the anchor atop Pitch 2 to a ledge just above the ground. If you have a shorter rope, rappel to the top of Pitch 1, then walk off.

**3    Solar Slab Gully (5.3)** A great excursion for the novice climber. Most climbers use this as an approach to *Solar Slab*. The route can be rappelled with one rope, and all of the anchors are fixed. The crux section is a short waterfall (usually dry) near the top. Start at the base of an obvious gully about 100' right of a prominent, right-facing corner system (*Beulah's Book*) and 200' left of a freestanding pillar (*The Friar*). **Pitch 1 (5.1)**: Start at the right-hand chimney, near a small oak tree. Climb straight up a varnished 8- to 12-inch-wide crack, passing ledges at 40' and 80', to yet another ledge with a tree and fixed piton. 150'. **Pitch 2 (fourth-class):** From the anchor, scramble up the bush-filled gully, then angle up left along ledges past a gnarled oak tree with rappel slings (80'). Continue up to a huge alcove at the base of a dark, water-worn chimney. 130'. **Pitch 3 (5.1)**: Climb straight up the black gully/corner and belay on a ledge to the left, just above a chockstone with numerous slings around it. About 60' up the pitch, you pass a rappel anchor made from a natural thread. 100'. **Pitch 4 (third-class)**: A short and easy chimney leads to a tree in a corridor. 40'. **Pitch 5 (5.3)**: Walk up the corridor, then ascend a 20-foot waterfall **(5.3)** to a bolt and piton. Scramble up the gully to the huge terrace. 120'. **Descent:** Rappel the route.

**4    Solar Slab (5.6 PG)** If you do this one in the summer, it would be best named "Sizzle Slab." This is a long route, so start early and move fast. Bring a good assortment of gear. This route is on the white face above *Solar Slab Gully*, so the approach entails climbing up to about 5.3 in difficulty. It is an enjoyable excursion for the novice climber. The gully is about 500' long and the most difficult section is near the top. There are fixed anchors up the gully because it is a standard descent route. The gully ends on a large terrace below the white *Solar Slab* and takes roughly 90 minutes for most parties to climb. **Pitch 1 (5.5)**: Begin on the terrace about 100' up and left from the top of *Solar Slab Gully*. This terrace is below a white slab and an obvious hand crack that doesn't reach the

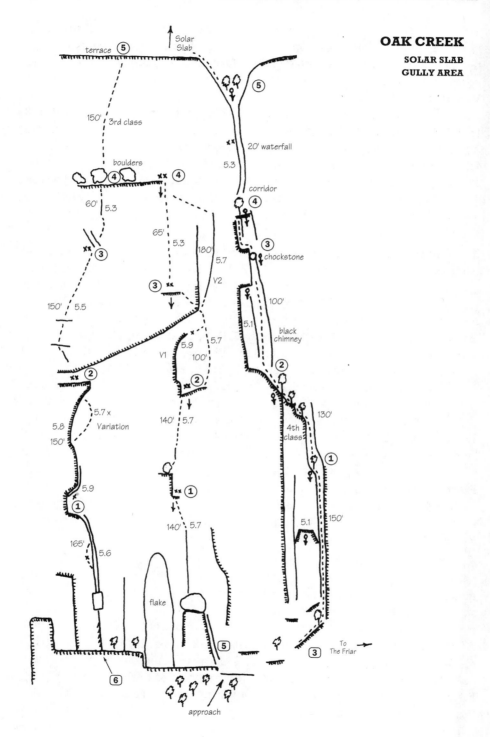

terrace. Climb the slabby face to varnished plates left of the crack. Eventually step right into the crack and follow it to a belay ledge with a prominent bush. 165'. **Pitch 2 (5.5)**: Follow the left-leaning ramp/chimney, passing a ledge about 90' up (possible belay here). Continue up the corner above, to belay on a ledge with a dead tree. 165'. **Pitch 3 (5.6)**: Traverse right 15', then climb a finger-and-hand crack to a ledge. Traverse right 10' and follow a small, right-facing corner to a belay stance (#2.5 and #3 Friends and small wires). 130'. **Pitch 4 (5.6)**: Traverse 10' right and climb a left-facing flake/corner (tricky) to a ceiling. Step down and right to a belay ledge. 150'. **Pitch 5 (5.5)**: Climb the obvious hand crack directly above, belaying at a stance in the crack (if you have a 60-meter rope, you can combine this pitch with the next). 150'. **Pitch 6 (5.4)**: Continue up the crack, which becomes a right-facing corner. Belay at the pillar's top. 60'. **Pitch 7 (5.3)**: Angle right across a white face to an obvious low-angle crack. Climb the crack to a ledge, then move right 10' and climb a right-facing corner to a huge terrace. 150'. **Pitch 8:** Walk and scramble up easy slabs (or see variation) to the base of a varnished, left-leaning dihedral. 150'. **Pitch 9 (5.5)**: Climb the corner to the top. 100'. **Variation:** If time is short, you can avoid the final pitch by traversing right around the outside corner, then scrambling to the top. **Descent:** There are several options. 1) The climb has bolted rap stations (set up for two 50-meter ropes) starting about three-fourths of the way up Pitch 7. The rap line goes straight down the face (not down the route), so you won't be able to see the rap stations as you climb. The last two pitches do not have bolted rap stations. If you wish to top out, either downclimb Pitch 8 and Pitch 9, or scramble back left to the top of Pitch 7 via the variation. 2) Walk about 800' up easy slabs to the bright, red rock. Head right (east) and enter a huge gully system. Do two or three rappels depending on your downclimbing ability. The descent can be done unroped, if you can solo down 5.6. In winter, the gully may contain ice and snow because it is in the shade all day. The bottom of the descent gully is about 400' right (east) of the base of *Solar Slab Gully*. 3) For another alternative descent, head down left (west) at the red rock and down into the Painted Bowl.

**5    Johnny Vegas (5.7)**  This sunny route has become very popular and rightly so. Bring wires, TCUs, cams up to #3, and two ropes. Start atop a white pillar 25' left of *Solar Slab Gully*. This pillar is just right of a 60-foot-high white flake leaning against the cliff. Scramble up to a stance just below the summit boulder of the pillar and rope up. **Pitch 1 (5.7)**: Climb the vertical crack system that is 10' left of a dihedral. Follow the crack to its top, then angle up and left across varnished plates. Belay at an anchor at the base of an obvious right-facing corner. 130'. **Pitch 2 (5.7)**: Climb the varnished right-facing corner above the belay to its top. Go up and slightly right to reach a vertical varnished

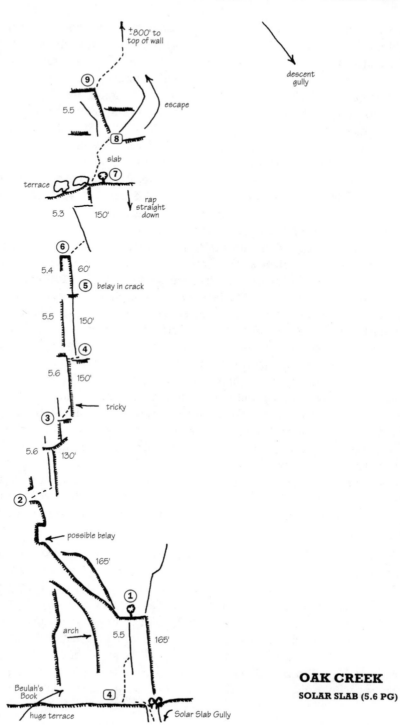

±800' to
top of wall

descent
gully

escape

5.5

slab

terrace

rap
straight
down

5.3        150'

5.4     60'

belay in crack

5.5        150'

5.6        150'

tricky

5.6        130'

possible belay

165'

arch

5.5       165'

Beulah's
Book

huge terrace          Solar Slab Gully

**OAK CREEK**

**SOLAR SLAB (5.6 PG)**

crack. Continue straight up the face from the top of the crack to a belay anchor on a sloping ledge. 140'. **Pitch 3 (5.7)**: From the belay, go up and right (see Variation 1) onto obvious varnished plates near the arête. Climb the arête past the right side of a huge roof, then angle back out left above the roof (see Variation 2) to a ledge and an anchor. 100'. **Pitch 4 (5.3)**: Climb the easy face to another anchor at the edge of the huge terrace. 65'. **Variation 1 (5.9)**: The original route went up the right-facing corner above the belay, then traversed right to the arête. Watch out for rope drag! **Variation 2 (5.7)**: Instead of angling back out left above the roof, follow the obvious right-leaning crack. You eventually exit left onto the face and up to the anchor atop Pitch 4. 180'. **Descent:** Rappel the route with two ropes.

**6     Beulah's Book (5.9-)**  One of the early chapters of this book deals with off-widths. Bring lots of gear up to a #4 Camalot. For fast parties, it's possible to combine this route (or *Johnny Vegas*) with *Solar Slab* to give nearly 1,500' of great climbing. Start 100' left of *Solar Slab Gully* at a series of dihedrals. This climb begins at the dihedral with a large, jammed block about 20' up and an oak tree growing out of the corner's base. **Pitch 1 (5.6)**: Climb the dihedral past the jammed block (possible belay), then climb the narrow face just left of the chimney past a bolt. Step back right into the chimney and follow it to a ledge. 165'. **Pitch 2 (5.9-)**: Continue up the corner/chimney system, passing a flaring bomb bay section (bolt, #4 Camalot) to the base of an obvious layback corner. Power up the 5.8+ corner (or see Variation) to a ceiling, then step left to a belay ledge in white rock. 150'. **Pitch 3 (5.5)**: Wander up the white face, angling slightly right to eventually belay at some left-leaning cracks. 150'. **Pitch 4 (5.3)**: A short, easy pitch leads up to a huge ledge with large boulders on it. 60'. **Pitch 5 (third-class)**: Scramble up slabs to the huge terrace where *Solar Slab* starts. 150'. **Variation (5.7 X)**: It is possible to climb the face to the right of the corner. **Descent:** Either descend *Johnny Vegas* (two ropes needed) or *Solar Slab Gully* (one rope needed).

## Eagle Wall Area

This sunny wall sits high up on the right (north) side of Oak Creek Canyon and is best viewed from around the First Creek trailhead. Take the north fork of Oak Creek Canyon, then follow a huge ramp up and right (northeast) to the bases of the routes. Total approach time is about 2 hours.

**7     Rainbow Buttress (5.8 PG)**  A great route, but with the long approach and descent, you'll need to move fast! Bring a good selection of gear for the belays as well as the climbing (including extra #3.5 and #4 Friends for Pitch 6). From The Wilson Pimple, follow the old roadbed and/or trail toward the canyon until the trail drops into the streambed. Hike up Oak Creek Canyon for about 1

hour until it splits. Continue up the right (north) fork until a huge, slabby ramp leads back up right toward the huge cliffband on the right. It is probably best to leave your pack here. Follow the ramp up (east; some cairns) for about 15 minutes to the base of the route. Start at the very top of the huge approach ramp about 400' uphill from *Levitation 29* and left (west) of Upper Painted Bowl. **Pitch 1 (5.4)**: Climb a shallow, varnished, left-facing corner that leads to a wider section of crack. Angle right across the white face to a belay ledge. Bring friends for the belay. 80'. **Pitch 2 (5.8)**: A good pitch. Climb the corner to a huge ledge (5.6), then continue up the left-facing corner to a big ledge with a bush. Nuts and the bush form the belay. 100'. **Pitch 3 (5.7)**: Swim up the off-width above (5.7), then up a corner system to a chimney. Exit right out of an alcove onto the face, then up the main, right-facing corner system to a belay ledge that is 20' below a bush. TCUs for the belay. 110'. **Pitch 4 (5.5)**: Climb the corner system past a ledge with bushes to a chimney, which leads to the top of The Black Tower. Slings around the summit of the tower and a #3 Friend form the belay. (Note: *Ringtail*, a 5.10 described in the Urioste guidebook, climbs the left side of the tower and terminates at this point.) 90'. **Pitch 5 (5.6)**: Step across from the top of the tower to a crack, then traverse 15' right to a right-facing corner. Climb this for about 40', then traverse 40' right across a slab to the base

# OAK CREEK CANYON

**EAGLE WALL**

**LEVITATION 29 AREA**

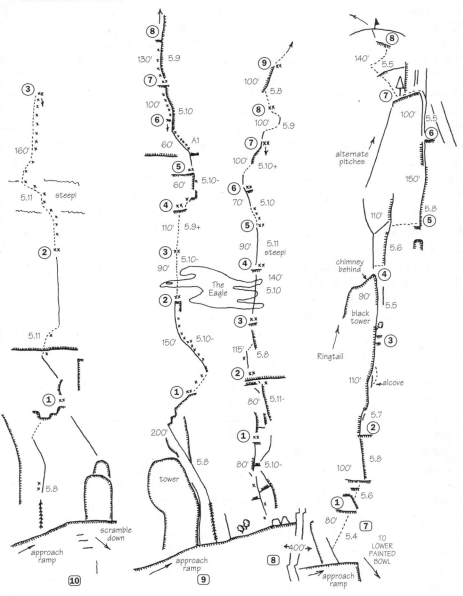

of an obvious left-facing corner. Belay in the corner (#3.5 and #4 Friends) at a point about 30' above a huge pedestal. 110'. **Pitch 6 (5.8 PG)**: Climb the obvious left-facing corner past a scary stemming section, a fist crack, and numerous bushes in a chimney. Belay above on a large ledge. 150'. **Pitch 7 (5.5)**: Continue up the easy, loose, and low-angle crack/chimney system to a huge, sloping ledge with a pine tree. Belay from the tree. 100'. **Pitch 8 (5.5 X)**: Climb the lower-angle face to the left of a left-facing corner, angling up and left to a ledge. Wander up and right to a belay on a terrace 50' below the summit. 140'. **Descent:** Scramble about 100 yards up toward the canyon rim, then contour left (west). Aim for ramps that lead toward a large, red pinnacle at the right edge of a red blob on the canyon rim. Go around the right (north) side of the pinnacle and blob, then follow a trail down along the canyon rim to the top of the Oak Creek drainage. This should take about 30 minutes. Follow the drainage down and east (toward the road) past numerous waterholes to the base of the approach ramp, a huge pine and your packs. From the top of the route, it should take about 1 hour to reach your pack at the base of the ramp.

**8    Levitation 29 (5.11 PG)** Considered by many to be the best route at Red Rocks. The climb is on a section of cliff that gets sun all day and is visible from the road. Bring lots of quickdraws and the usual assortment of wires, TCUs, and Friends up to #3. From The Wilson Pimple, follow the old roadbed and/or trail toward the canyon until the trail drops into the streambed. Hike up Oak Creek Canyon for about 1 hour until it splits. Continue up the right (north) fork, until a huge, slabby ramp leads back up right toward the huge cliffband on the right. Follow the ramp (some cairns) to the base of the route, which is about 400' down from the ramp's top and about 200' right of a huge, black pillar where some varnished cracks lead to a giant roof about 100' up. **Pitch 1 (5.10)**: Climb thin, varnished cracks past 4 bolts to an anchor. 80'. **Pitch 2 (5.11)**: Move right, then go up to the roof. Fire this (bolts) and belay up and left from bolts. 80'. **Pitch 3 (5.8)**: Climb a crack for 75', then angle up right past bolts to a bolted belay at a stance. 115'. **Pitch 4 (5.10)**: Follow a crack up the face past 7 bolts to an anchor just below a steeper section of the wall. 140'. **Pitch 5 (5.11)**: The pumpfest. Follow the obvious crack and 13 bolts to a bolt anchor. 90'. **Pitch 6 (5.10)**: Climb seams up left past 5 bolts to the fixed belay. 70'. **Pitch 7 (5.10+)**: Pussyfoot up and left along a white, rounded seam to a depression. A bit of power liebacking gets you up the right edge of the depression and to the safety of the belay anchors. 100'. **Pitch 8 (5.9)**: Go up and right to a thin crack. When it ends, go left to a belay on a slab. 100'. **Pitch 9 (5.8)**: Climb up and right along corners and cracks to a right-slanting, right-facing corner. Belay from 2 bolts, after clipping 7 on the pitch. 100'. **Pitch 10 (fourth-class)**: Some fourth-class climbing leads to the top of the wall. **Descent:** Many people rappel with two ropes after the seventh pitch. If you elect to hike down, walk left (west) along the top of the wall, curving around left (south) onto white rock. Follow the ridge and slabs down left to the top of the Oak Creek drainage. It should take about 30 minutes from the summit to the top of Oak Creek Canyon. Follow the drainage down and east (toward the road) past numerous waterholes.

**9   Eagle Dance (5.10- A0)** This route and the formation are named for the likeness of a huge eagle (flying west) formed by desert varnish in the center of the wall. This climb goes through the eagle's neck, and *Levitation 29* goes through the tail. The climb is on a section of cliff that gets sun all day and is visible from the road. Bring lots of quickdraws, lightweight aiders (or long slings), and the usual assortment of wires, TCUs, and Friends up to #2.5. From The Wilson Pimple, follow the old roadbed and/or a trail toward the canyon until the trail drops into the streambed. Hike up Oak Creek Canyon for about 1 hour until it splits. Continue up the right (north) fork until a huge, slabby ramp leads back up right toward the huge cliffband on the right. Follow the ramp (some cairns) to the base of the route. Start at a shallow, varnished dihedral about 50' right of a huge, black pillar that rests against the cliff. This is about 450' down from the very top of the approach ramp. **Pitch 1 (5.8)**: Climb the dihedral and crack above to a belay ledge with bolts. This ledge is about 30' above the top of the black pillar. 200'. **Pitch 2 (5.10-)**: Move right and climb past 2 bolts (use long slings); follow a seam up left past 8 more bolts (and a possible belay) to a belay stance atop a block at bolts. 150'. **Pitch 3 (5.10-)**: Fly straight up the white face, passing through the eagle's neck and 13 bolts. Belay at a stance with a bolted anchor. 90'. **Pitch 4 (5.9)**: Nine more bolts lead up to a bolt belay on a sloping ledge. 110'. **Pitch 5 (5.10-)**: Move up right past 1 bolt to a ledge at the base of a short, left-facing corner. Climb up loose flakes and a right-facing corner (bolt) to a stance with bolts. 60'. **Pitch 6 (5.8 A0)**: Follow a thin crack up to a bulge, then thrash and dangle out the bulge (8 bolts) to a crack and the belay anchor. 60'. **Pitch 7 (5.10)**: Follow the corner/groove and 7 bolts to the next anchor (on a ledge). 100'. **Pitch 8 (5.9)**: Go up and left in a corner past 4 bolts to a ledge. 130'. **Pitch 9:** Scamper up a corner to the top. **Descent:** There are two options. Rappel the route with two ropes from the top of Pitch 7, or, walk left (west) along the top of the wall, curving around left (south) onto white rock and follow the ridge and slabs down left to the top of the Oak Creek drainage. It should take about 30 minutes from the summit to the top of Oak Creek Canyon. Follow the drainage down and east (toward the road) past numerous waterholes. You eventually exit the drainage on its right (south) bank and follow a trail and the old road back to your vehicle. If you parked on the spur road, exit left (north) out of the drainage to return to your car.

**10   Dances with Beagles (5.11)** Bring gear up to a #1.5 Friend, at least 17 quickdraws(!), and two ropes for the rappel. From The Wilson Pimple, follow the old roadbed and/or  trail toward the canyon until the trail drops into the streambed. Hike up Oak Creek Canyon for about 1 hour until it splits. Continue up the right (north) fork until a huge, slabby ramp leads back up right toward the huge cliffband on the right. Follow the ramp (some cairns) to the base of the route. Start about 300' left (west) of *Eagle Dance* at a point 40' left of a 50-foot-high pillar. This is just right of a huge, varnished, left-facing corner. **Pitch 1 (5.8)**: Climb an easy, varnished dihedral to a steep seam/crack. Follow the seam/crack past 2 bolts then continue up and slightly left along the fissure to its end. Go up and right to a ledge with an anchor. 140'. **Pitch 2 (5.11)**: Follow a flake above the belay to a thin, left-leaning seam in very smooth rock. Climb the seam and ceiling above (bolt) to an easier face. Move up and right (bolt) to a thin, varnished crack, which is followed to a 2-bolt belay stance. 130'. **Pitch 3 (5.11)**: Follow 17 bolts up the steep face above, belaying at a 2-bolt stance. 160'. **Descent:** Rappel the route using two ropes.

CHAPTER TEN

# Black Velvet Canyon

Black Velvet Canyon is home to the most famous and classic routes at Red Rocks. The approach hike isn't too long (compared to some of the other canyons) and is actually quite enjoyable. To reach the trailhead, you must drive west on Nevada 160 for 4.6 miles (from the intersection with Nevada 159) to a dirt road. If you reach mile marker 16, you have gone too far. The dirt road is not marked by a sign, so keep your eyes open!

Turn right (north) at a cattle guard and follow the dirt road 1.9 miles from

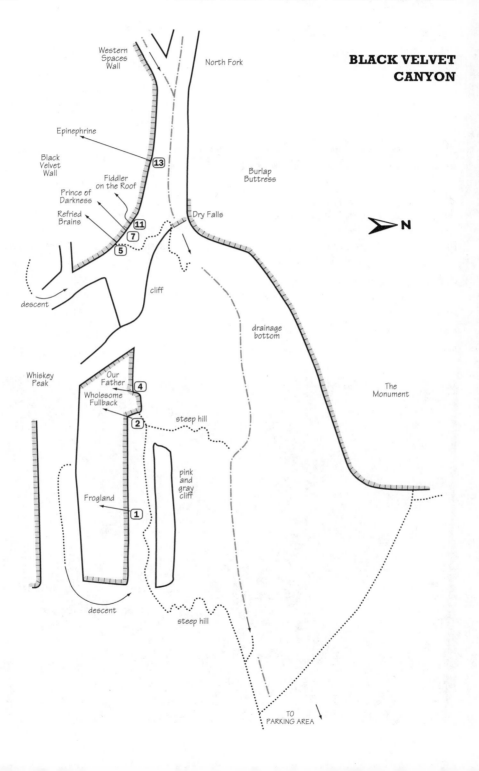

Frogland Area

NV 160 to the third dirt road on the left. Make this left turn, drive another 0.5 mile to a T-intersection, then turn right and drive 0.3 mile to the parking areas at the end of the road. To get here, you'll be driving on rough dirt roads, but there is no need for a special type of vehicle. To continue beyond the normal parking areas (to which there is no real benefit), you'll need four-wheel-drive.

As of press time, there was a distinct parking area at the end of the passable road, and the BLM did not allow camping here. There is no water, trash pickup, or bathrooms, so please do your part to keep this area clean and unpolluted. Again, if we don't police ourselves, there could be major repercussions!

## *Whiskey Peak*

The next routes described are on the left (south) side of the canyon on Whiskey Peak. These routes are generally shady.

**1     Frogland (5.8-)**   The sustained nature of the route may keep you hopping! Bring a good selection of gear because all of the pitches are long and wander a bit. Follow the roadbed about 300 yards from the parking area, then take a trail that branches off right where the road makes a hard left turn. Hike this trail for about 0.5 mile, until it forks. Take the left trail (the right fork drops down a hill into the main drainage) for another 200 yards until you are on a red dirt ridge. Follow a faint trail steeply uphill, headed for the left (east) edge of an obvious red and pink rock band below the main canyon wall. Once atop the rock band, contour right (west) about 200 yards to the base of the route. The approach takes about 30 minutes. Start at a clearing on a ledge 100' right (west) of a huge, white section of cliff. Between the white section of rock and this route are numerous crack systems filled with bushes and trees. The first pitch of this route ascends a left-facing corner system with a large, white flake at its base. **Pitch 1 (5.7)**: Scramble atop a block, then climb a left-facing dihedral past 3 bolts to an obvious sapling. Continue up to the highest ledge with oak bushes on it. 140'. **Pitch 2 (5.6)**: Climb a beautiful low-angled dihedral above to a ledge (80'). Continue straight up the chimney/flake (or see Variation) to another ledge just below a prominent, bushy ledge. 150'. **Pitch 3 (5.6)**: Pull a small ceiling, then angle left under the bushy ledge to the main dihedral. Follow this to a bulge, then move right and up to a belay stance in a varnished, left-leaning corner. 150'. **Pitch 4 (5.8-)**: Angle left across the varnished face to a ledge. Climb the low-angle white dihedral to a bolt, then continue up 8' to a ceiling. Finger-traverse straight left to the arête, then up a thin crack to a stance. Continue up the face and shallow dihedrals above to a stance at a bush. 150'. **Pitch 5 (5.8-)**: Face-climb up white rock to a bolt, then angle up left into a chimney with a huge chockstone jammed in it. Tunnel easily underneath the chockstone, then step right above it and pull past a white bulge to belay in the easy chimney above. 150'. **Pitch 6 (5.6 PG)**: Scamper up the chimney a bit, then angle right out on the face. Follow thin cracks up to a ceiling and move back left to the corner and a bushy ledge. 120'. **Pitch 7 (fourth class)**: Scramble up any of the easy routes to the top of the buttress. 100'. **Variation:** The original route traversed left to a corner, then went up that to rejoin the line described here. **Descent:** From the top of the buttress, head left (east) down a

## BLACK VELVET CANYON

**FROGLAND (5.8-)**

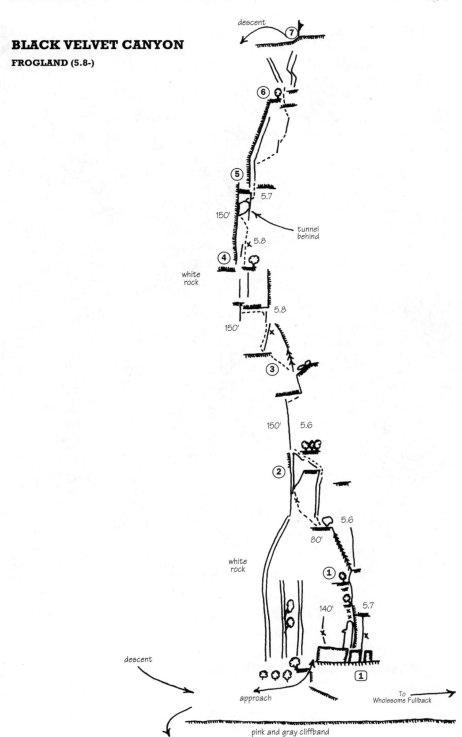

descent

7

6

5

5.7

150'

tunnel behind

5.8

4

white rock

5.8

150'

3

150'  5.6

2

5.6

80'

white rock

1

1

5.7

140'

descent

approach

To Wholesome Fullback

pink and gray cliffband

Wholesome
Fullback

Descent Route

To Road

gully toward the road. There are three gullies leading down; take the rightmost (southern) one, then contour back around to the base of the route. This is very simple and surprisingly quick.

**2     Wholesome Fullback (5.10-)** An excellent route that can be done to round out your day. Bring gear up to a #4 Friend, with emphasis on the 1" to 3" sizes. This route can be approached by following the roadbed for about 300

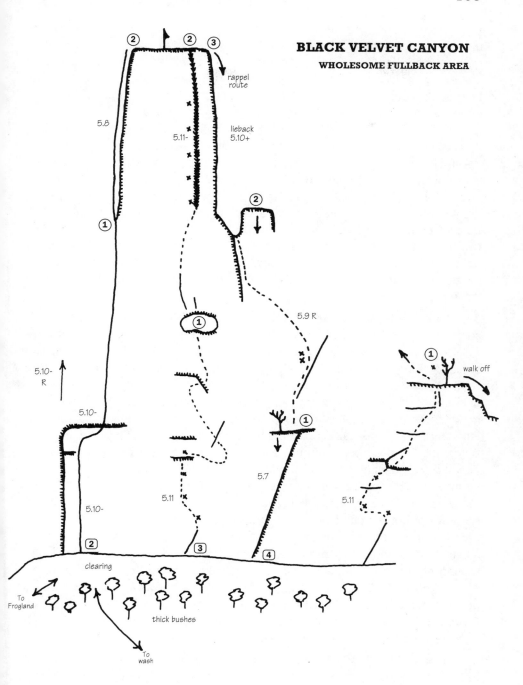

**BLACK VELVET CANYON**

WHOLESOME FULLBACK AREA

yards from the parking area, then taking a trail that branches off right where the road makes a hard left turn. Hike this trail toward the canyon for about 0.5 mile, until it forks. Take the right fork and drop down into the drainage. Follow the rocky creekbed upstream for about 300 yards, until you reach a trail leading steeply up left (south). Take this trail up, skirting the right (west) edge of a pink rock band below the main canyon wall. You should now be roughly below *Wholesome Fullback*, which climbs the left side of a prominent pillar that only goes partway up the cliff. The approach takes roughly half an hour. Begin about 10' right of a right-facing corner, below an obvious finger crack in a brown, varnished slab. **Pitch 1 (5.10-)**: Climb the slabby face to reach the crack, then follow this past a ledge to an overhang. Jog right (or see variation), then continue up the crack to a belay at the base of a chimney. 150'. **Pitch 2 (5.8)**: Follow the chimney to the top of the pillar. 100'. **Variation (5.10- R)**: At the point where *Wholesome Fullback* moves right, climb straight up the face for a full pitch. You eventually move back right to the top of the tower. **Descent:** Go down *Our Father* on the right (west) side of the pillar in three short rappels.

**3     The Delicate Sound of Thunder (5.11 PG13)**   As awesome as it sounds! Not for the faint of heart. Your rack should include a bit of gear up to a #2 Friend. This route is best approached by following the road from the parking area for about 300 yards, then taking a trail that branches off right where the road makes a hard left turn. Hike this trail toward the canyon for about 0.5 mile, until it forks. Take the right fork and drop down into the drainage. Follow the rocky creekbed up for about 300 yards, until you reach a trail leading steeply up left (south). Take this trail up, skirting the right (west) edge of a pink rock band below the main canyon wall. You should now be roughly below *Wholesome Fullback*, which climbs the left side of a prominent pillar that only goes partway up the cliff. This approach should take about 30 minutes. Start about 50' right of *Wholesome Fullback* at a short, small, right-leaning corner. This left-facing corner is about 10' left of *Our Father*. **Pitch 1 (5.11 PG13)**: Wander up the face past 4 bolts, making difficult moves past the second bolt. Traverse right from the fourth bolt, making 5.10 moves way out. Climb up to a ceiling, then swing around right and up the face to an alcove (funky anchors, nothing good fixed). 140'. **Pitch 2 (5.11-)**: Climb a short crack above the alcove, then continue up the obvious arête past 5 bolts to the top of the pillar. Excellent positions! 100'. **Descent:** Rappel down *Our Father* on the right (west) side of the pillar in three short rappels (only one rope needed).

**4     Our Father (5.10+ R)**   Say your prayers before leading the second pitch! Bring extra 2" to 3.5" gear. This route is best approached by following the road from the parking area for about 300 yards, then taking a trail that branches off right when the road makes a hard left turn. Hike this trail toward the canyon for

Black Velvet
Wall

up canyon

about 0.5 mile, until it forks. Take the right fork and drop down into the drainage. Follow the rocky creekbed up for about 300 yards, until you reach a trail leading steeply up left (south). Take this trail up, skirting the right (west) edge of a pink rock band below the main canyon wall. You should now be roughly below *Wholesome Fullback*, which climbs the right side of a prominent pillar that only goes partway up the canyon wall. This approach takes about 30 minutes. Begin

**BLACK VELVET CANYON**

**REFRIED BRAINS (5.9)**

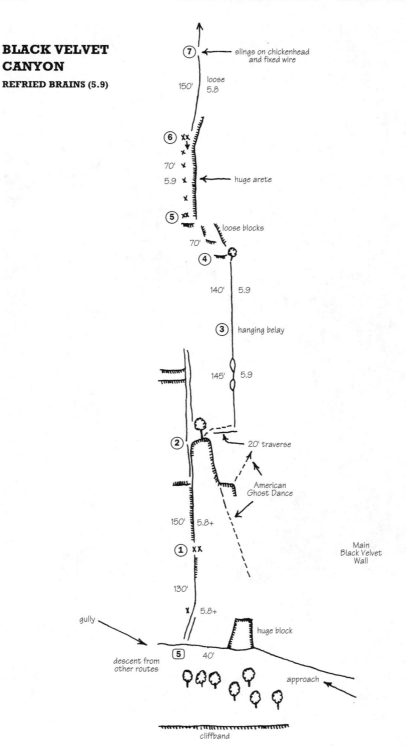

slings on chickenhead and fixed wire

loose 5.8
150'

huge arete
70'
5.9

loose blocks
70'

140'   5.9

hanging belay

145'   5.9

20' traverse

American Ghost Dance

150'   5.8+

130'

5.8+

gully

huge block

descent from other routes

40'

approach

Main Black Velvet Wall

cliffband

60' right of *Wholesome Fullback* at a right-leaning crack/corner and below a prominent, white, right-facing corner marking the right side of a pillar leaning against the main canyon wall. **Pitch 1 (5.7)**: A fun pitch in itself. Climb the right-leaning crack/corner to a belay ledge with a tree. 60'. **Pitch 2 (5.9 R)**: Climb up the face to double bolts, then angle left into the obvious right-facing corner. Belay above, atop a block (fixed anchor). 100'. **Pitch 3 (5.10+)**: Jam and lieback up the perfect right-facing corner above. 50'. **Descent:** Do three short rappels (only one rope needed) to get down.

## Black Velvet Wall *(see photo page 105)*

The next routes are on the Black Velvet Wall. This wall is separated from Whiskey Peak by a series of large gullies. These routes are described from left to right and are in the shade most of the day (all day in the winter).

**5      Refried Brains (5.9)** A good pun—the route is OK, too. Bring two ropes to rappel the route and large gear for the wide cracks. Approach this climb by following the road for about 300 yards from the parking area, then take a trail that branches off right where the road makes a hard left turn. Hike this trail toward the canyon for about 0.5 mile, until it forks. Take the right fork and drop down into the drainage. Follow the rocky creekbed upstream for about 600 yards until the drainage is blocked by a cliff/waterfall. Go left (southeast) into the bushes on a path, then scramble up the cliff on big ledges. Follow the trails up left about 100 yards to the base of the large, smooth wall. This section of cliff has some of the best routes in all of Red Rocks. Plan on 30 minutes for the approach hike. Start about 40' left of a huge block leaning against the base of the crag. **Pitch 1 (5.8+)**: Climb a crack up and right past a bolt to reach an obvious crack. Follow this to a small left-facing corner. At the top of the corner, step left to a belay below a prominent, right-facing corner. 130'. **Pitch 2 (5.8+)**: Step left, then climb up via face, crack, and a right-facing corner (the last 20' of which becomes a chimney/slot). Stretch the rope to belay atop a pillar at the "tree-of-a-thousand-slings." 160'. **Pitch 3 (5.9)**: Traverse straight right on a shelf for 20' to a crack. Follow this up past a couple of off-width sections to a hanging belay in the crack. 145'. **Pitch 4 (5.9)**: Continue up the crack system to a small tree with slings. Wander up and left past blocks to an obvious bolted belay on the arête. 140'. **Pitch 5 (5.8)**: Face-climb up and left (keeping left of the arête), then straight up past 3 bolts. Turn a bulge on the left (bolt), then up and right to another bolted belay. 60'. **Pitches 6–7 (5.8)**: These are best avoided because the rock deteriorates, and there are poor fixed anchors atop Pitch 6. If you want to continue, follow cracks to the top of the pillar. **Descent:** Rappel the route with two ropes, at times using anchors other than those used for belays on the ascent.

**6     Rock Warrior (5.10 R)** A classic route, but **lots** scarier than *The Prince of Darkness*. Bring a selection of smaller-size gear, two ropes, and a cool head. Approach this route by following the roadbed for about 300 yards from the parking area, then take a trail that branches off right where the road makes a hard left turn. Hike this trail toward the canyon for about 0.5 mile, until it forks. Take the right fork and drop down into the drainage. Follow the rocky creekbed upstream for about 600 yards until the drainage is blocked by a cliff/waterfall. Go left (southeast) into the bushes on a path, then scramble up the cliff on big ledges. Follow the trail up left about 100 yards to the base of the large, smooth wall. This section of cliff has probably the best long routes in all of Red Rocks, including this one. It takes roughly 30 minutes to reach the route from your car. Rope up at a smooth, varnished face to the right of a low ceiling and left of a short pillar forming a left-facing corner. This is 30' left of *Dream of Wild Turkeys* and *The Prince of Darkness*. **Pitch 1 (5.10- R)**: Climb 40' up and right on white rock (easy, but dangerous) to a slab. Clip a bolt, climb up, and traverse right until beneath the anchor. Climb up past 1 more bolt and make sporty moves to reach the belay. 150'. **Pitch 2 (5.10)**: Angle slightly left from the belay to a bolt, then wander straight up to another bolt by a shallow, left-facing corner. Make difficult moves up the arête of the corner to a seam, which is followed up and slightly right past a bit more fixed gear to the anchor. 150'. **Pitch 3 (5.10- R)**: Go slightly left from the belay, then up the face, past a little bit of fixed gear to a ceiling. Pull this and move up to a belay station. 150'. **Pitch 4 (5.9 R)**: Wander up the face to a 3-bolt belay at a corner (the first ascent party bivied here in hammocks). 150'. **Pitch 5 (5.9 R)**: Climb the corner, then up the face past a few bolts to another station. 150'. **Pitch 6 (5.10- R)**: Climb over a ceiling, then up along cracks and seams to a belay. 150'. **Descent:** Either continue up (5.8/5.9, then third class) or rappel with two ropes.

**7     The Prince of Darkness (5.10c)** This route is impressive—not only for the positions you'll be in, but for the amount of effort needed to drill all the bolts you'll encounter (some say it's overbolted). Bring lots of quickdraws, a few medium-sized stoppers, butt bag (all the belays are hanging belays), and two ropes for the descent. The bolt hangers are painted black, as the route name might imply (ominous, eh?). Approach this route by following the roadbed for about 300 yards from the parking area, then take a trail that branches off right where the road makes a hard left turn. Hike this trail toward the canyon for about 0.5 mile, until it forks. Take the right fork and drop down into the drainage. Follow the rocky creekbed upstream for about 600 yards until the drainage is blocked by a cliff/waterfall. Go left (southeast) into the bushes on a path, then scramble up the cliff on big ledges. Follow the trail up left about 100 yards to the base of the large, smooth wall. This section of cliff has some of the best routes in all of Red Rocks. *The Prince of Darkness* follows the left edge of a prominent,

# BLACK VELVET CANYON

### BLACK VELVET WALL

### (NOT ALL BOLTS SHOWN.)

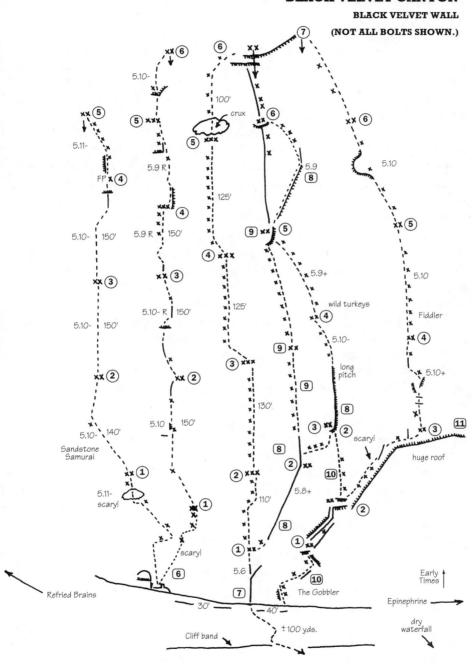

5.10-

100'

crux

5.11-

FP

5.9 R

5.10-  150'

5.9 R  150'

5.10-  150'

5.10- R  150'

5.10  150'

5.10-  140'

Sandstone
Samurai

5.11-
scary!

scary!

Refried Brains

125'

125'

130'

110'

5.6

30'

Cliff band

5.9

5.9+

wild turkeys

5.10-

long
pitch

scary!

5.8+

5.10

Fiddler

5.10

5.10+

huge roof

The Gobbler

40'

± 100 yds.

Early
Times

Epinephrine

dry
waterfall

black waterstreak in the center of the smooth wall. Approach time is about 30 minutes. Same start as *Dream of Wild Turkeys*, below the left end of an obvious, right-leaning crack 100' up and directly below a right-facing crack/corner about 40' up. **Pitch 1 (5.6)**: Scamper up easy rock to the base of a short, right-leaning crack/corner with a vertical crack leading straight up. Follow either feature up to a slab and a belay station with 3 bolts. 75'. **Pitch 2 (5.10b)**: Follow a crack/seam system up, then slightly right, passing 14 bolts to a 3-bolt belay station. 110'. **Pitch 3 (5.10a)**: Continue straight up the seam past 15 bolts to a 3-bolt belay. 130'. **Pitch 4 (5.9)**: Zip up along the crack past 13 bolts (at least 2 are missing hangers) to a 3-bolt belay. 125'. **Pitch 5 (5.9)**: Step left, then follow a crack past 8 bolts to a 3-bolt belay. 125'. **Pitch 6 (5.10c)**: Power up the smooth, varnished slab (crux) past 13 bolts to a large ledge and a 2-bolt belay (same belay as *Dream Of Wild Turkeys*). 100'. **Descent:** Rappel this route, *Yellow Brick Road*, or *Dream of Wild Turkeys* with two ropes.

**8     Dream of Wild Turkeys (5.10-)**     One of the earliest routes up this section of cliff. The name is a goof on a famous climb located on a sea cliff in Wales *(Dream of White Horses* on Wen Slab). Bring an assortment of gear up to a #3 Friend and two ropes to rap the route. Approach this climb by following the roadbed from the parking area for about 300 yards, then taking a trail that branches off to the right when the road makes a hard left turn. Hike this trail toward the canyon for about 0.5 mile, until it forks. Take the right fork and drop down into the drainage. Follow the rocky creekbed upstream for about 600 yards until the drainage is blocked by a cliff/waterfall. Go left (southeast) into the bushes on a path, then scramble up the cliff on big ledges. Follow the trail up left about 100 yards to the base of the large, smooth wall. This section of cliff has some of the best routes in all of Red Rocks. Give yourself about 30 minutes to reach the base of the wall. Same start as *The Prince of Darkness*, below the left end of an obvious right-leaning crack 100' up and directly below a right-facing crack/corner about 40' up. **Pitch 1 (5.6)**: Scamper up easy rock to the base of a short, right-leaning crack/corner with a vertical crack leading straight up. Follow either feature up to a slab and a belay station with 3 bolts. 75'. **Pitch 2 (5.8+)**: Angle right past a bolt into the prominent right-leaning crack and follow this to a belay anchor. 110'. **Pitch 3 (5.9)**: Go up the crack a bit, then traverse right past 6 bolts to the base of a prominent, white flake/corner system and the belay anchors. 80'. **Pitch 4 (5.10-)**: Climb the flake/corner system to its end (5.8), then face-climb left past bolts to a bolt anchor. 165'. **Pitch 5 (5.9+)**: Angle up left across a slabby face (6 bolts) to a ledge at the base of a left-facing corner. 50'. **Pitch 6 (5.9)**: Follow the left-facing corner/ramp up right to a crack. Go up the crack and face above (bolts), then traverse back left (more bolts) to a vertical crack in a waterstreak. Belay from 2 bolts on a scooped ledge. 140'. **Pitch 7 (5.9)**: Climb the left-slanting crack/seam past 5 bolts to a spacious ledge with 2 bolts. 75'. **Pitches 8–12:** It's possible to continue up, but most folks rappel from here. **Descent:** Rappel with two ropes, using anchors on *Yellow Brick Road* and/or this route.

**9      Yellow Brick Road (5.10)** You don't need to be a wiz to know that the bolt hangers are painted yellow on this one. Really a 3-pitch variation to *Dream of Wild Turkeys*; the climbing is safe and enjoyable. Start at the base of *Dream of Wild Turkeys* and *The Prince of Darkness* below the left end of an obvious, right-leaning crack 100' above and directly below a right-facing crack/corner about 40' up. **Pitch 1 (5.6)**: Scamper up easy rock to the base of a short, right-leaning crack/corner with a vertical crack leading straight up. Follow either feature up to a slab and a belay station with 3 bolts. 75'. **Pitch 2 (5.8+)**: Angle right past a bolt into the prominent right-leaning crack and follow this to a belay anchor. 110'. **Pitch 3 (5.10b/c)**: Continue straight up the crack and face above to a hanging belay from bolts. 120'. **Pitch 4 (5.10a/b)**: Follow 10 bolts up the face to rejoin *Dream of Wild Turkeys* at a belay station. 125'. **Pitch 5:** Ascend the left-facing flake to a bolt, then move left and up a crack/corner (2 more bolts) to a 2-bolt belay on a scooped ledge. **Descent:** Either continue up *Dream of Wild Turkeys* or rappel the route with two ropes.

**10      The Gobbler (5.10-)** A good way to round out the day or start *Dream of Wild Turkeys*. Make sure you have some long slings and gear up to 3". This route is best approached by following the road from the parking area for about 300 yards, then taking a trail that branches off right when the road makes a hard left turn. Hike this trail toward the canyon for about 0.5 mile, until it forks. Take the right fork and drop down into the drainage. Follow the rocky creekbed upstream for about 600 yards until the drainage is blocked by a cliff/waterfall. Go left (southeast) into the bushes on a path, then scramble up the cliff on big ledges. Follow the trail up left about 100 yards to the base of the large, smooth wall. It'll take about 30 minutes to reach the base of the route from the parking area. Start below a right-leaning gash about 60' up (rappel anchors are clearly visible) and 40' right of *Dream of Wild Turkeys*. This climb is at the left (east) end of a huge arch/ceiling at the base of Black Velvet Wall. **Pitch 1 (5.9)**: Climb easy white rock for 30' to a bolt in a depression. Go up left 10' to another bolt then up to a horizontal break. Move up right past 2 bolts, then finger-traverse up right to a left-leaning crack/corner. Follow this past a bolt to a ledge and belay station (watch out for rope drag). 110'. **Pitch 2 (5.10-)**: Jam up cracks just right of the right-leaning gash/chimney past 1 bolt to another anchor (5.9, possible belay here). Power up the steep face past more bolts to a belay on *Dream of Wild Turkeys* at the base of a white, left-facing flake/corner system. 130'. **Descent:** Either continue up *Dream of Wild Turkeys* or rappel the route. Watch out for ropes stuck in the cracks!

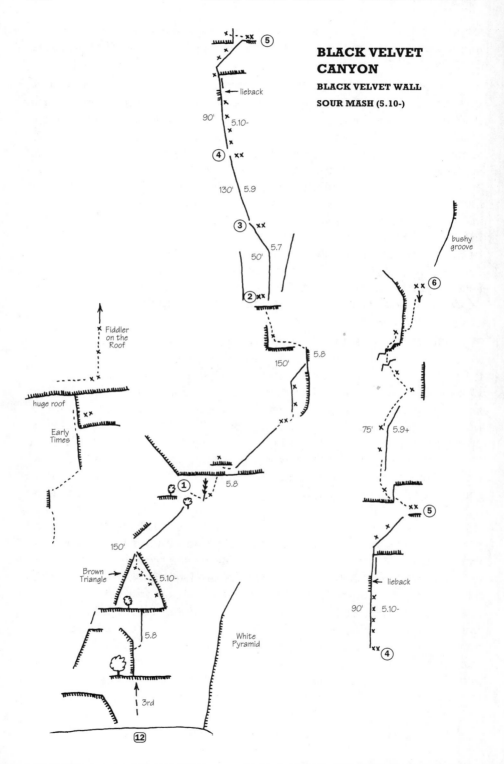

**BLACK VELVET CANYON**

**BLACK VELVET WALL**

**SOUR MASH (5.10-)**

**11    Fiddler on the Roof (5.10+ PG13)** Bring your prussiks! This exciting route starts at the second anchor on *The Gobbler* and traverses out right above the lip of the huge arch/ceiling. Rumor has it that 1 or 2 bolts have been added to the route, which could make it less sporty than the protection rating implies. Start below a right-leaning gash about 60' up (rappel anchors are clearly visible) and 40' right of *Dream of Wild Turkeys*. This climb is at the left (east) end of a huge arch/ceiling at the base of the Black Velvet Wall. **Pitch 1 (5.9)**: Climb easy white rock for 30' to a bolt in a depression. Go left 10' to another bolt then up to a horizontal break. Move up right past 2 bolts, then finger-traverse up right to a left-leaning crack/corner. Follow this past a bolt to a ledge and belay station (watch out for rope drag). 110'. **Pitch 2 (5.9)**: Jam up cracks just right of the right-leaning gash/chimney past 1 bolt to another belay anchor. 60'. **Pitch 3:** Trend out right along the lip of the huge roof (don't fall!), passing 2 bolts and a few gear placements to a belay station. 165'. **Pitch 4 (5.10+)**: Climb pretty much straight up the spectacular face past 2 bolts to a bolted belay. 150'. **Pitch 5 (5.10)**: Continue up the magnificent varnished face, past 6 bolts and some traditional gear placements. Fixed anchor. 150'. **Pitch 6 (5.10)**: Follow 2 bolts up the face to a ledge **(5.10)**, then continue up past 1 more bolt to the belay. 150'. **Pitch 7:** Two more bolts lead to Turkey Ledge. **Descent:** Rappel *Dream of Wild Turkeys* with two ropes.

**12    Sour Mash (5.10-)** A primarily natural line up the wall just right of the huge arch mentioned in *Fiddler on the Roof* and *The Gobbler*. Carry a good selection of pro and two ropes. Access this climb by following the roadbed from the parking area for about 300 yards, then taking a trail that bnches off to the right when the road makes a hard left turn. Hike this trail toward the canyon for about 0.5 mile, until it forks. Take the right fork and drop down into the drainage. Follow the rocky creekbed upstream for about 600 yards untithe drainage is blocked by a cliff. Go left (southeast) into the bushes on a path, scramble up the cliff band as pethe other routes, then go up to the base of the wall on one of the trails. Total approach time is about 30 minutes. Begin below the right end of the huge roof and just left of a large, white, pyramid-shaped buttress. The route ascends the right side of a brown triangle of rock about 60' up, then follows crack systems that keep right of the huge roof. Scramble 20' up to a ledge with a bush. **Pitch 1 (5.10-)**: Climb up a shallow, right-facing corner, then step right and go up a steeper lieback crack to a ledge with a bush. Climb the left-facing corner/crack above (this is the right side of the brown triangle) past bolts to the top of the triangle. Follow an easier, right-leaning crack/corner to a belay stance between two bushes. Large Friends are needed for the belay. 150'. **Pitch 2 (5.8)**: Move right from the belay to an arête, then up this past a bolt to the ceiling. Pull the first ceiling to a second bolt, then follow a crack up and right to a belay anchor (possible belay here). Continue up a crack past 2 bolts. Step

left on a ledge to a bolt, then up 20' to another ledge with a bolted anchor. 150'.
**Pitch 3 (5.7)**: Climb the center of three crack systems above to a hanging
belay. 50'. **Pitch 4 (5.9)**: Follow the crack up and slightly left to a hanging belay.
130'. **Pitch 5 (5.10-)**: Continue up the obvious, slightly left-leaning seam/crack
past bolts to a stance. Lieback a flake up a smooth section past a small ceiling,
then angle up and right to a 2-bolt belay anchor below another light-colored
ceiling. 90'. **Pitch 6 (5.9+)**: Step over the ceiling to a bolt. Face-climb along a
crack past 2 bolts to a smooth section. Make difficult moves past bolts to a left-
facing corner. Step right and up to a rappel anchor. 75'. **Descent:** Rappel with
two ropes straight down to *Fiddler on the Roof*'s belay at the lip of the huge roof.
Another wild rappel and a bit of downclimbing return you to the base of the
route.

**13     Epinephrine (5.9)** One of the best climbs I've done, but you'd better be
solid on 5.9 chimneys! A long route with sustained climbing and lots of third-
and-fourth-class scrambling to get off. The pitches are described as they were
originally done, but it's entirely possible to combine pitches (especially above
the top of the tower) to make the climb go faster. Approach this fine outing by
following the roadbed from the parking area for about 300 yards, then taking a
trail that branches off to the right when the road makes a hard left turn. Hike this
trail toward the canyon for about 0.5 mile, until it forks. Take the right fork d drop
down into the drainage. Follow the rocky creekbed upstream for about 600
yards until the drainage is blocked by a cliff/waterfall. Go left (southeast) into the
bushes on a path, scramble up the cliff as for the other routes, then go right and
down to the pebbly streambed. Approach time is about 40 minutes. *Epinephrine*
is 60 yards up-canyon from the waterfall and starts below a gray face with 3
bolts (red hangers), which is 15' right of a right-slanting crack. If speed is a
consideration, you can avoid the first pitch by starting 50' farther right and
soloing up easy ledges (30' left of a yellow, left-facing corner, which is the line of
*Texas Hold'em*). **Pitch 1 (5.8)**: Climb the gray face past 3 bolts to a bushy ledge.
60'. **Pitch 2 (5.7)**: From the left side of the ledge, follow the obvious features up
and slightly left past 3 bolts to another vegetated ledge. 100'. **Pitch 3 (5.6)**:
Climb an easy chimney and belay above at one of many trees. 150'. **Pitch 4:**
Scramble up to the base of the chimneys, which are on the right side of the huge
pillar (The Black Tower). **Pitch 5 (5.9)**: Struggle up the beautiful chimney to a
belay station. 150'. **Pitch 6 (5.9)**: Continue up the chimney to another anchor
(awesome positions). 75'. **Pitch 7 (5.9)**: Another pitch of wiggling and thrashing
leads to the chimney section's top. 90'. **Pitch 8:** Scramble to the top of the tower.
(Note: The top of the tower is quite spacious, leans inward, and is really the only
place to bivy. Many folks climb to here, then rappel back down the route. The
rappels down the chimney are set for two 60-meter ropes.) **Pitch 9 (5.7)**: Face-
climb past 2 bolts to a belay. 75'. **Pitch 10 (5.7)**: Pull a ceiling, then go up to a

# BLACK VELVET CANYON

**BLACK VELVET WALL**

**EPINEPHRINE (5.9)**

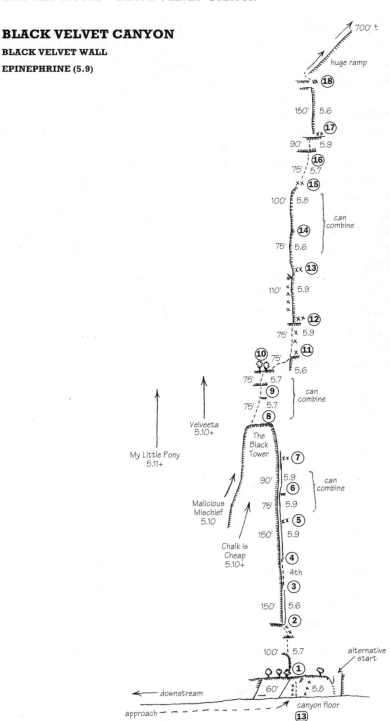

bushy ledge. 75'. **Pitch 11 (5.6)**: Traverse right about 50', then climb up to a belay ledge with 1 bolt. 75'. **Pitch 12 (5.9)**: A bit of tricky face-climbing past 2 bolts leads to another belay ledge. 75'. **Pitch 13 (5.9)**: Climb the prominent dihedral past 5 bolts to a belay in an alcove. 110'. **Pitch 14 (5.6)**: Continue up the dihedral to belay on a ledge. 75'. **Pitch 15 (5.8)**: Upward! 100'. **Pitch 16 (5.7)**: More of the same. Belay under a roof. 75'. **Pitch 17 (5.9)**: Climb the roof on the right (exposed), then up to a belay anchor. 90'. **Pitch 18 (5.6)**: Up! Belay on a ledge to the left under a ceiling. Bolt anchor. 150'. **To the top:** Move left from the belay onto a huge, right-leaning ramp (many large ledges to organize on). Follow this ramp up right for about 700', passing numerous places where folks have had to bivy (some for the second time!). This involves fourth- and easy fifth-class climbing, sometimes with big air below. The last bit of the route follows bushy ledges around an amphitheater to the top of the wall. **Descent:** Walk up and left (south) to the highest summit (don't be lured down the first gully you come to), then follow the ridge down to the top of Whiskey Peak (you'll be heading down toward the parking area). From the top of Whiskey Peak, drop down into the left (northwest) gully and scramble down past *Refried Brains* and the other routes to your pack. To the right (southeast) from the top of Whiskey Peak is the fastest way to the car, if you have all of your gear with you. The whole descent takes roughly an hour (if you have something other than your tight climbing shoes with you!).

# ROUTES BY GRADE INDEX

*= highest quality*

## 5.12c

## 5.12d

## 5.13a

## 5.13b

# ROUTES BY NAME INDEX

# ACCESS: It's every climber's concern

**The Access Fund,** a national, non-profit climbers' organization, works to keep climbing areas open and to conserve the climbing environment. Need help with closures? land acquisition? legal or land management issues? funding for trails and other projects? starting a local climbers' group? CALL US!

Climbers can help preserve access by being committed to leaving the environment in its natural state. Here are some simple guidelines:

• **STRIVE FOR ZERO IMPACT** especially in environmentally sensitive areas like caves. Chalk can be a significant impact on dark and porous rock—don't use it around historic rock art. Pick up litter, and leave trees and plants intact.

• **DISPOSE OF HUMAN WASTE PROPERLY** Use toilets whenever possible. If toilets are not available, dig a "cat hole" at least six inches deep and 200 feet from any water, trails, campsites, or the base of climbs. *Always pack out toilet paper.* On big wall routes, use a "poop tube" and carry waste up and off with you (the old "bag toss" is now illegal in many areas).

• **USE EXISTING TRAILS** Cutting switchbacks causes erosion. When walking off-trail, tread lightly, especially in the desert where cryptogamic soils (usually a dark crust) take thousands of years to form and are easily damaged. Be aware that "rim ecologies" (the clifftop) are often highly sensitive to disturbance.

• **BE DISCREET WITH FIXED ANCHORS** *Bolts are controversial and are not a convenience*—don't place 'em unless they are *really* necessary. Camouflage all anchors. Remove unsightly slings from rappel stations (better to use steel chain or welded cold shuts). Bolts sometimes can be used pro-actively to protect fragile resources—consult with your local land manager.

• **RESPECT THE RULES** and speak up when other climbers don't. Expect restrictions in designated wilderness areas, rock art sites, caves, and to protect wildlife, especially nesting birds of prey. *Power drills are illegal in wilderness and all national parks.*

• **PARK AND CAMP IN DESIGNATED AREAS** Some climbing areas require a permit for overnight camping.

• **MAINTAIN A LOW PROFILE** Leave the boom box and day-glo clothing at home—the less climbers are heard and seen, the better.

• **RESPECT PRIVATE PROPERTY** Be courteous to land owners. Don't climb where you're not wanted.

• **JOIN THE ACCESS FUND!** To become a member, make a tax-deductible donation of $25 or more.

# The Access Fund

*Preserving America's Diverse Climbing Resources*
PO Box 17010 Boulder, CO 80308
303.545.6772 • www.accessfund.org